A DETECTIVE'S STORY

A DETECTIVE'S STORY

Stories from the life of a Policeman
in British India

David Marsh-Smith

ISBN: 1-903314-05-4

Printed in Wales
by Gwasg Pantycelyn, Caernarfon

ACKNOWLEDGEMENT

My thanks to my wife and daughter Lucy for their skillful use of a word processor in preparing the typescript.

*   *   *

For my grandchildren

CONTENTS

PREFACE 9

INTRODUCTION 11

THE SAVING OF GANDHI 13

AN AMBUSH 18

DOG'S WORK - PART I 24

DOG'S WORK - PART II 31

A TRIO OF INCIDENTS 38

SHER SINGH - DACOIT LEADER 43

A TALE OF TWO HEADS 50

MOB-HYSTERIA 64

WE LAUGH LAST 74

AN INSIDE JOB 83

IT MIGHT HAVE BEEN DIFFERENT 103

THE PERFECT CRIME 112

FOR GALLANTRY 123

    A Butcher's Butchery 123

    Saved by a Dog 125

    Thanks to the Sentry 126

    The Sadhu was a Bad Shot 127

    A Lucky Silhouette 127

AN ENGLISHMAN'S THOUGHTS ON INDIA

I have a love for India,
The land where I had my birth,
I have a passion for India,
Her vastness, her grandeur, her worth.

I've spent a life-time in India,
I know of her joy and her pain,
I have been long years in India,
I know of her loss and her gain.

I owe a debt to India,
A debt I can never repay,
I've eaten the salt of India,
To that salt I'll be true alway.

I owe a duty to India,
To help her with all my might,
I'll take a vow for India,
To her my troth I'll plight.

I have a fear for India,
That she may be a prey to strife,
I have a dread for India,
Lest she thus imperil her life.

I have a hope for India,
That she may be prosperous, happy, and free,
I have a vision of India,
Of her greatness about to be.

I have a prayer for India,
That my fear and dread may be wrong,
I ask God's blessing for India,
That my hope may prove true ere long.

11-3-46.   R.N.M.S.

8

PREFACE

My father, Rex Marsh-Smith, went out to India (United Provinces) in 1911 to serve as a police officer. He married the daughter of a senior Civil Service officer in 1919. He served mainly in the U.P. until the war which saw him as Secretary to the Government dealing with food rationing and Air Raid Precautions. He was appointed Companion of the Star of India and Companion of the Indian Empire. He ended his career as Inspector General of Police Gwalior (Madhya Bharat). He investigated the murder of Gandhi but so quick was he to uncover the plot that he was accused by Nehru of being involved!

Coincidentally it was his father-in-law who years earlier had proposed Nehru's father for the Club in Allahabad. Unfortunately he was black balled which led to the Nehru family becoming anti-British.

The main part of this book consists of edited versions of his accounts of his detective and administrating activities mainly in the U.P. He was much involved in the capturing of dacoits, the murderous gangs engaged in burglary and theft. Normal police activities such as tracking down murderers and thieves and keeping order in the towns also kept him occupied.

Several attempts on his life led to his receiving three medals for gallantry. In the last chapter I describe some of these. He compared himself to a cat having nine lives.

He was devoted to India and an enthusiastic supporter of the Indians' aspirations for independence.

David Marsh-Smith

INTRODUCTION

Service in India in the days before the grant of independence to the two new countries, India and Pakistan, provided an infinity of experiences to the many Britishers who sought service there. This book relates some of the experiences which occurred in the life of one who had the good fortune to serve there in a minor capacity as a district official. The period of these incidents, 1911 to 1948, was certainly the most momentous in modern India.

The period opened with the Delhi Durbar which King George the Fifth held to mark the transfer of the capital of India from Calcutta to Delhi, and the grant of considerable advance towards self-government, as embodied in the Morley Minto Reforms. It ended with fulfilment of the promise made from time to time to make India independent, and the near-consummation of all the hopes of Indian patriots for the last one hundred years. Circumstances have prevented the full consummation of those hopes, in that there is not one united free India, and the sub-continent has been divided into two sovereign countries, free from outside control and from each others' control.

In writing these reminiscences which set out some incidents and experiences in the life of a British official, I have been moved by a desire to pay some small tribute to my own memories of a land to which I owe so much. The stories are anecdotes of incidents which occurred within my own ken. In most of them I figure personally, and some of them I appear as the central figure, but that is inevitable when relating personal experiences. The stories are all founded on fact, but some alterations have been made of happenings and names of places, as well as the sequence of events. The stories have no connection, one with another, and are not intended to point any moral or illustrate any feature of conditions in India, or in the Police in particular. If during the relation of any incident, anything apparently disparaging has been included, it should not be interpreted as indicating that any adverse characteristic was common to all members of the Police Force. It cannot be claimed that the Police Force in any part of India approached perfection or obtained the standards of efficiency reached in western countries. But it is claimed that considering the difficulties of the conditions, and the handicaps in the way of finance and equipment the Police Force throughout India reached a degree of efficiency fully commensurate with the general standard of administration in the country. It is further claimed that these Police Forces worked with the utmost loyalty to the Government of the day, a tradition which they are continuing in relation to the present Governments of India and Pakistan.

Rex Marsh-Smith

THE SAVING OF GANDHI

Mohan Chand Karam Gandhi, better known as Mahatma Gandhi, was the great Indian Nationalist who, after studying law in London and practising as a barrister in Bombay, went to South Africa where he spent many years fighting for the improvement of the treatment accorded to his countrymen there. He came to India in 1919, and immediately became leader of the Nationalist Movement which had been started by a political organisation known as Congress. Its avowed object was the termination of British rule in India. It was first styled the Non-co-operation Movement but in later years was given the title of the Civil Disobedience Campaign which was to reach culmination after the second World War in the partition of the country into two independent States, now known as India and Pakistan.

Mahatma Gandhi and Pandit Jowahir Lal Nehru, the first Prime Minister of India, formed the two-pronged spearhead of the movement which was responsible for achieving this result.

The incident which I now relate occurred almost twenty years before that most momentous event in the history of the sub-continent. It occurred during a comparatively quiet period in that turbulent struggle between the Congress and the then Government of India. Gandhi had been arrested in 1922 on a charge of sedition and had been sentenced to six years imprisonment, but in 1924, having served only two years, he was released. He very soon resumed his political activities and actually he was again arrested in 1930. In the meantime he was stumping the country holding meetings and stirring up the people but keeping within the law. He quickly acquired a large following and everywhere he went huge crowds invariably gathered to welcome him and listen to his speeches; great crowds always flocked to the railway station (this was before the general use of the motor car which enabled such journeys to be made by road). In the course of his fresh campaign he was scheduled to visit Cawnpore almost at the height of his popularity. I was in charge of the Police Force of that district, and was, under control of the District Magistrate, responsible for the maintenance of law and order.

At this stage of the campaign, the form the agitation would take, and its reaction among the public, were imponderables. In some places in India his visit had led to commotions and riots involving clashes with the Police and considerable bloodshed. It was, of course, our intention to try to avoid any such happenings in Cawnpore.

It had been my practice to establish as friendly relations as were consistent with control, with the local leaders in these movements. In this way we were able to keep in touch with their intentions; admittedly we were sometimes led up the garden path by these gentlemen. However, on the whole, the system worked and it was in pursuance of this policy that I agreed to receive a deputation from the local Congress leaders to discuss the arrangements for the Mahatma's visit. On this occasion, they wanted to make a somewhat novel proposal for the start of the visit. This is what they proposed:

"Sahib", they said, "We have a request to make. It is this – that you leave the arrangements for the Mahatma's actual arrival at the station to us. We want to receive him as he steps out of the train and offer him "daishan" (a sort of adulatory welcome involving much bowing and scraping and touching of hands and foreheads). We will offer him our daishan and then escort him to the house of our President. You will, of course, take over responsibility as soon as he comes out of the station".

Perhaps somewhat unwisely, I agreed to this request and left it to the Congress leaders to make the arrangements on the platform. I persuaded the Station Master, who was basically responsible within the station, to agree, and there we left it. I was only too pleased not to have to supply extra policemen to help the Railway Police on the platform.

Had this arrangement with the Congress leaders not been made, entrance to the platform would have been strictly controlled, and only a handful allowed in to meet the Mahatma. The leaders had intimated that they wanted to admit a somewhat larger number than usual. I supposed that there would be perhaps one hundred persons allowed in.

The train was due to arrive about 3 p.m. – fifteen hours in railway parlance. It was, I remember, a particularly hot day, and I felt sure that only a small number would want to undergo the discomfort of the stifling heat. I figuratively sat back and relaxed in my office – glad of the opportunity to get rid of some arrears of routine work.

However I was to be sadly disappointed. At about 2.30 p.m. I got a telephone message from the Railway Police Station to say that large crowds were assembling at the station. Later, another message said that entrance to the platform was not being controlled. I did not consider that anything untoward was likely to happen. Perhaps three or four hundred people would get on to the platform. They would not be in any way a hostile crowd and would not represent any danger to the Mahatma. They would all be his followers. All they would do would be to raise repeated cries of "Jai Mahatmaji" (long live Mahatma!). He would descend from his carriage, the leaders would do daishan and then escort him to his conveyance and he would drive off to the house where he was to stay.

The Railway Police messages were not in any way alarming, nevertheless I thought I had better go along to see what was happening; so, accompanied by two orderlies, I drove down to the station. What I saw there was altogether unexpected. Literally thousands of Congressmen were hastening to the station, and there was a huge concourse of Hindus, wearing white Gandhi caps, and most of them clad in Khaddar (home-spun cotton clothes). They were perfectly orderly except that they were uttering Congress cries and slogans. "Boycott British goods", "No co-operation with the Angrazi Raj", Gandhi ki jai", "Jawahar Lal Nehru ki jai", "Vidyarthi ki jai" (the local leader), but the real trouble was that far too many persons had been admitted to the platform.

15

On arrival at the station I was met by the leaders – they were flushed with excitement, but jubilant. Their welcome to Gandhiji was going to be a success beyond their wildest dreams. I expressed some concern at the dense crowd on the platform, but they said that they had a sufficient number of young men (styled 'volunteers') who were keeping order and would easily hold back the crowds. They begged me not to interfere at this late stage: their welcome would be spoilt if the police took over.

I sized up the situation and decided that to take over at this stage and disperse the crowd on the platform would not only require quite a number of policemen (far more than were present on duty) but it would also turn a perfectly peaceful concourse into a hostile mob with all its possible consequences of a breach of the peace, and a serious riot. So I agreed to let Congress carry on.

Shortly afterwards, the train came in. I decided to await events sitting in my car outside. As the train steamed in, the air was rent with deafening cries of "Mahatmaji ki jai" – which went on for ten minutes or so. All seemed to be going well when suddenly there arose a great wailing cry "Mahatma margya" – the Mahatma has been killed!

Indeed, this appeared to be confirmed when two of the leaders came running to my car – "Sahib, Sahib come quickly". I leapt out of my car and fought my way through struggling crowds towards the train. There I found that Gandhiji had been crushed by the onrush of the adoring crowd and had slipped down between the train and the platform. All the Congressmen had lost their heads and just did nothing to rescue him from his plight. He was, indeed, in considerable danger, especially as the train staff were anxious to get on with the journey, as they were already late. They were not aware of what had happened and the guard was blowing his whistle. There was no time to lose – so I sprang forward and grabbed the Mahatma's hand. He was wearing only a "dhoti" and the upper part of his body was bare. It was difficult to get a grip on him but I managed to pull him free, not without causing him some painful scratches and bruises.

He weighed less than a hundred pounds, so I picked him up and perched him on my shoulder for all the crowd to see. Once again there was a deafening tumultuous cry, this time of Joy. "Mahatmaji ki jai" – and to my surprise "Kaptan Sahib ki jai" (the district Chief of Police was always known as "Kaptan Sahib).

As for Gandhiji – he said "Sahib, you have saved my life. How can I ever thank you properly." I carried him to my car and we drove to his residence where we had a cup of tea.

That is the story of how I was able to render a service to the great Nationalist who was such an embarrassment to the British Raj in ensuing years.

But perhaps the strangest part of my story is that twenty years later it was alleged that I had taken part in the conspiracy which resulted in his dastardly assassination in Delhi in the first year of independence. But that is another story.

AN AMBUSH

"Sahib, there's a man who wants to see you personally". Thus spoke the Office orderly one day as I was sitting in my office.

"Well what sort of a person is he? Anyhow, bring him in".

"But he says he wants to see you in secret, alone".

So I cleared my office and sent for the caller. He was, by all appearances, an ordinary village cultivator, but I soon learnt from him that he was a member of a gang of dacoits. Dacoit gangs are formed under some wild ruffian leader, and they swoop down at dead of night on the house of some wealthy man in the village. They are generally armed with lathis (long stout bamboo sticks) but some will have swords or spears, while the leader, and perhaps one or two others, will have firearms of varying degrees of modernity and accuracy. They enter their victims' house by climbing the wall into his courtyard, or battering down his front door. They then plunder the house, after torturing the inmates to get them to disclose where the valuables are hidden away. The more profligate among them will molest the woman of the house. Technically or legally, a dacoity is a robbery committed by five or more than five persons.

Well, my caller was a member of one of these gangs, and, as so often happens, he was displeased with the other leaders of the gang because he had not been given what he considered was his fair share of the loot. He had joined in their last dacoity with a single barrelled muzzle-loading gun, and was therefore entitled, according to all the cannons of dacoit gangs, to a double share. The fact that he did possess a firearm was an indication that he was one of the important members of the gang. He came now to lay information about the gang, with a view to getting them caught by the police.

"But why did you not go to the nearest thana (police station) and tell the Darogha (the officer-in-charge)"?

"What would have been the use, Sahib? Pirbhoo, our leader, pays the thana staff one hundred rupees a month to purchase immunity. The darogha would merely have sent word back to Pirbhoo that I had split, and my life would not have been worth living. Pirbhoo would have got me bumped off within a week".

"So that's how the land lies" I said to myself, thinking of the good reputation the darogha had built up for himself, and how my leg was being pulled by him and his subordinates. Well, that made the matter of catching the gang far more difficult as I could not use the local police and must keep them in ignorance of any plan to catch the gang.

Fortunately the informer said the gang was going out that very day to commit a dacoity in the neighbouring police circle to that of the corrupt darogha with the good reputation. (These clever station officers never allow a dacoity to be committed in their own circle). The gang, in order to get to the scene of their intended attack, would have to cross the main canal (fifty yards wide) by a bridge about fifteen miles from our headquarters. It was arranged that we should try to ambush them as they crossed over the canal bridge.

Those were the days of very little motor transport, and the police used to move in horsedrawn vehicles, or more often, on their flat feet. There was just time, however, to get a party of police to the other side of the canal by a circuitous route. I sent for one of my best havildars (sergeants of the armed police) – a real tough guy who played centrehalf for our police hockey team.

"Shafti", I said, "you have just got time to take your jowans (young men) to a spot near the Rajpur bridge. You must lie up in a place near the bridge, and must not on any account be seen even by the inhabitants of the nearby village; otherwise news will be carried to the police station of your coming. I expect the gang to cross the bridge about half an hour before midnight. You must gradually move nearer to the bridge so as to be in a position to cut them off absolutely when they come across. We will endeavour to come up behind them from our side. You will not be able to communicate with us, so you will have to disclose your presence there somehow".

"That is alright," said Shafti, "There is a recruit under training in the Lines who is an Aheria (a sort of natural hunter; they generally live in Jungle villages). He can imitate the call of a pea-fowl. When we get into position, he will give a pea-fowl's call a few times, and by that you will know we are in position".

"Good. Take him with you – but there's yet another difficulty. You will not be able to take any guns with you, for if you fire, we shall also be in your line of fire, and might get hit as easily as the dacoits. No, you will have to trust to lathis. So will we, for that matter, in case we should hit you".

"That's grand", said Shafti. "My lads have not yet learnt how to use their rifles properly but they do know how to use lathis".

"Right, now's your chance, take your lathis and use them. The dacoits may have guns, but we have got to risk that. Get off at once. I am afraid you and your jowans must miss your khana (dinner) and you'll get nothing till we get back".

Shafti went off, mightily pleased with his assignment. He was as tough as old boots, and was training his lads to become the same.

Meanwhile I told another havildar, my personal head orderly, to collect another lot of selected jowans who would go with us. I sent the informer off to get back to his gang.

"Don't you worry, Sahib", he said, "they'll come along all right, but, mind you, they'll fight if they are cornered, and may use guns, but they only have muzzle-loaders".

Prior to coming to see me, he had learnt the whole plan of the gang and was sure he could bring them to the point of ambush.

We got hold of four one-horse traps (ekkas) and duly set out with my orderly and his bunch of jowans, and a trusted sub-inspector from the city police. It was necessary to arrive in the area in the dark and to abandon our vehicles and march stealthily, under cover wherever feasible, so as to get as near the bridge as possible.

To be seen by any of the villagers would have been fatal to the success of our scheme.

It took two hours to do the last three miles from the place where we had to leave our vehicles, but by great good fortune, we found a mango grove with a good deal of undergrowth within a stone's throw of the bridge. We were there about an hour before anything could happen. We all had to lie down concealed in the undergrowth. No standing up, no talking except in whispers, and of course, no smoking which we would gladly have indulged in, if only to keep the insects off our faces. Worst of all, no one must cough. It is generally a desire to cough which betrays the presence of people who want to hide their presence. It is almost inconceivably difficult to repress a desire to cough or clear one's throat, and it is a very high test of discipline.

We reached our point in the rendezvous without being seen, but what about the other party? Were they in their appointed place on the other side of the canal? We began to get worried on this score as zero hour drew near. Only a short time was left when, suddenly, in the stillness of the night, a pea-fowl began to call. It was almost too natural, but we knew that this was the lad, Rama Aheria. The other party had reached the rendezvous and our anxiety was relieved. On our side we had put out a few intelligent scouts – well hidden – but lads who could identify the informer. As the time drew near, excitement rose, especially for the lads who had never been in this sort of show before.

Suddenly somebody jumped down into our grove, almost on top of us. It was one of the scouts with the informer.

"They're just coming, huzur (your honour), but along the canal bank and not along the road. You must stay well hidden and very still because we will pass within a yard of you on the other side of the wall of this grove".

After hurriedly whispering this message, he slipped away without a sound. Soon after, we could see from our hide-out shadowy forms coming stealthily down the bank of the canal. I counted twenty three. Most of them had lathis, but one or two had spears. On they came, talking in low voices among, themselves, all unsuspecting the trap they were walking into.

We held our breath. We could see their faces as they passed. I could almost have touched some of them. Woe betide any of our party who stirred or coughed! But the whole gang passed quite unaware of our presence, and came on to the bridge.

This was our chance. We gave a loud shout (to attract our men on the other side) and charged in upon them up to the bridgehead. They started to run, only to find their way blocked on the other side. They became very excited, as they realised they had run into a trap.

I was at the head of the party. I alone had a gun, a sporting shotgun, which I levelled towards the gang, calling upon them to surrender.

Suddenly there was a flash and a report, and I received a charge of shot over my legs and hands; my gun in the levelled position saved my face. One of the dacoits had discharged a country made pistol, filled with shot. He then jumped on to the parapet of the bridge. At that moment the moon came out from behind a cloud, and I saw him leap twelve feet below into the water. As he hit the water, I fired my gun. He disappeared under the water, but in the moonlight my subinspector who had previously served in this circle, recognised him as the leader, Pirbhoo Nai. We made an immediate search on the banks of the canal but failed to find him. I dispatched the sub-inspector to his house in one of our traps. He arrived there just after Pirbhoo himself had reached his home in drenched clothes, and his back dripping with blood where my number four shot had hit him. He was, of course, arrested.

Meanwhile the rest of the gang, after putting up a stout fight, were overpowered, but three of them escaped through the cordon. The man with the pistol had swum under water for about two hundred yards and thus escaped our search.

We collected our bag and proceeded to march off home to our lines. Twenty dacoits arrested, with only a few bruises on our side besides the shot lodged in me. Some of the dacoits had been badly hammered by the jowans whose blood was up.

I called up Havildar Shafti. "Your men must be hungry", I said. "No, Sahib, it was meat and drink to them to get into the fight, and they've forgotten their hunger. Rama especially enjoyed himself knocking hell out of the dacoits, some of whom were of his own caste".

So we came home, highly pleased with our success, while I still carry on my hand and legs marks of the shot fired at me.

As for the corrupt darogha with good reputation, he got a very rude shock when the news reached him, and the explaining away of the existence of this gang ostensibly unknown to him, gave him a real headache.

Dog's Work – Part I

Little use has so far been made of dogs as detecting agents in India. This is largely due to climatic conditions – scent is quickly dispersed under atmospheric conditions which generally prevail over most parts of the country. Personally I consider that with a certain amount of planning, and in the light of the vast improvement in transport conditions, this handicap could be largely overcome. Soon air travel will come into the picture, and it may be possible to get a dog on to the scene in some of the remote parts of the country if only a landing ground is available. Further, the science of training and handling these dogs has advanced greatly. The breed of dog now generally put into training is more likely to stand up to severe conditions which prevail.

A present handicap is that evidence of a dog's actions (and the deductions to be drawn from them), are not considered expert evidence, and do not receive the unquestioning acceptance of other expert witnesses such as finger-print experts or medico-legal witnesses.

In most cases, when a dog has tracked the criminal, the latter's reaction is to give himself away by some significant remark or action, or more generally, to see that the game is up, and make a full confession. But in India the Law of Evidence lays down that no statement made to a police officer can be put in evidence against the accused who made it. The Indian police officer, when making an arrest, does nòt say "anything you say may be given in evidence".

This is, incidentally, one of the main handicaps under which the police in India have to work. This was, no doubt, against the intention of the original drafter of the Indian Evidence Act, and leads to the production of a great deal of faked evidence to bolster perfectly true cases,

Nevertheless even in the period of this story, (before 1914), we achieved some considerable success in spite of these various handicaps. The district concerned had been suffering from a spate of violent crime, particularly of dacoity (armed gang robbery). My chief at the time purchased, as a private venture, two trained bloodhounds. Their names were Horatio and Belinda. Unfortunately neither he nor I had any experience of using these dogs, and it was impossible to secure the services of a trained handler. There were, at that time, few Indians who could do this job. Largely because of religious and caste prejudices, only persons of low caste would handle dogs. Domestic dogs were always the charge of the lowest menial in the establishment, namely the sweeper, called euphemistically the "mehtar". We accordingly had to engage a sweeper to do the work, and as a matter of precaution, and for legal reasons, we enlisted him as a constable. This gave him the protection of the law in case he was attacked, and the power of arrest should he reach his quarry ahead of the accompanying police. However it was quite against the rules and regulations, as the enlistment of low caste persons into the police was at that time strictly forbidden. Naturally the sweeper selected had to be of specially good physique, and a picked man. Actually we succeeded in recruiting a genuine lover of dogs, and he handled our dogs with much skill and devotion. His name was Basanta, and although only twenty-four years of age, he had a wife and three children. As will be seen in the next story, it was fortunate that we succeeded in getting him the status of constable.

I well remember our first case because it proved a trying ordeal for dogs and men. It so happened that a dacoity was reported from a small hamlet about three miles from our house at the headquarters of the district.

My chief was delighted. "Here we are laddie", he said to me "Now's our chance to try the dogs".

At that time our faith in them had not been established, and we were only too painfully aware of our own ignorance and inexperience of handling them. We looked upon this as a trial which would probably fizzle out after a short run.

It was the beginning of the hot weather. Because of our ignorance and lack of faith, we omitted to make arrangements for liquid refreshments for ourselves, or, still worse, for the dogs. We were absolute novices at the job of handling them, but hoped to profit by our experience and rectify errors later. Accordingly, in some excitement, we repaired in a bamboo trap (no motors in those days!) to the scene of the dacoity, fortunately so near.

We found that the actual crime was not a very serious one; a comparatively minor bania (village trader) had been the victim. He had been robbed mostly of cooking utensils, and the women of the house had been stripped of their ornaments and trinkets. The victims could give but little information to establish the identity of their assailants. A ragged shirt, left behind by one of the gang, and the fact that cooked food had been taken away pointed to low caste thieves. Only the lowest cast of Hindus (the untouchables) could touch or eat cast-off food. But this at first did not help very much.

In India, except in the desert tracks, tracking by footprints in areas near towns and villages is extremely difficult because of the multiplication of tracks. Only in the event of a markedly peculiar footprint or shoe-print can success be obtained by human tracking, and reliance on the naked eye. In this case we should have been helpless without the dogs, for there had been a great deal of foot traffic near the scene, and the village cattle had all been led out to graze; the actual visible tracks of the gang had been practically obliterated.

Fortunately we reached the scene before the investigations had started and there was no fear of our being led astray by wrong evidence being given to us. After careful inspection of the scene we put both the dogs on the trail. They were helped by the scent from the old shirt left behind by the gang, but as the scent was comparatively fresh, they were mostly affected by the scent of the foot-tracks of the gang.

They quickly led off in the direction of the railway line which was half a mile from the village, and they followed the railway line for about four miles, avoiding all inhabited areas, The dogs seemed to get keener as they went, and they pulled us along almost at a trot. My chief and I each had a dog chain. He was getting on in years, and by the time we started to leave the railway line, he was done.

"I can't stick this pace", he said. "You carry on. I can't tell you how disappointed I am, because it looks as if we are on to something hot".

"Right Sir"! said I, but not feeling too good myself. "But I think we had better give the dogs a rest; they obviously want a drink".

So we called a halt, and sent off one of the policemen with us into a nearby village to get pitchers of water, and when he returned, the dogs drank greedily. As soon as they had quenched their thirst, they kept pulling at their chains to get us starting again. I foolishly tried to take both dogs but very soon had to give that up, as they pulled me along much too fast. So I took Horatio and Basanta the sweeper took Belinda.

On we went, leaving the railway line and going across country over a "usar" plain – land somewhat resembling desert land, in that it is not cultivatable. In some parts it is sandy but in general it is firm ground. Whenever we came to sandy patches, we came across footprints, mostly of bare feet, and these same prints kept on repeating themselves across miles of this "usar" ground. Some pieces of Chapatti (cooked Indian bread) and grains of cooked rice were found near the prints. We were clearly on the right track.

By the time we got across the "usar" to the sown area again the dogs were again showing signs of distress, especially Belinda. Fortunately we came to a stream and both dogs lay down and wallowed in the water. After some minutes, I decided to press on, but the bitch just could not do it and we had to leave her with a policeman to follow later in the cool of the evening.

On we went again. Horatio had quite recovered, but at the next village I took along with us a water carrier with his leather water-bag, and we sprinkled water on Horatio from time to time as we went along. We came to another stream. There were clear signs that the gang had halted here. Horatio would not stop even to drink. He started to tug at his collar and chain and to bay.

There was no village in sight in the direction in which we were being taken but as I peered around trying to divine the reason for the dog's excitement, I saw smoke rising from a small hill about two miles off. This could only mean that some wandering criminal tribe – similar to our gypsies – must have their encampment on the hill.

Our own excitement grew as Horatio dragged us towards this place. Clearly these must be the low-caste people who had committed the crime, and had stolen, among other things, cooked chapatties and rice. I did some rapid thinking. If, indeed, these were our quarry, when we got closer to their encampment, the gang would see that a police party was coming, and the men-folk, at least, would all decamp. So we halted and took cover.

I called up the police sub-inspector, who was with us, and said, "Daroghaji, if we go straight on, these Sansiahs will spot us and make off. We must somehow cut off their retreat. You must take a couple of constables to the village on our right, and quickly collect some villagers. You and the constable must discard your uniform, and your whole party must get round behind the hill, and pretend to be doing something in the fields until we come up. Then you must climb the hill and surround the camp. Hurry up, for the dog is getting impatient, and may start to bay again and thus give away our presence".

The sub-inspector hurried off with two constables. Fortunately there was sufficient cover for Basanta, myself and the dog, and we could not be seen from the camp. Horatio was only too keen to get on, and when we eventually set off, our suspicions that the track would lead to the camp soon proved correct. The dog started off at a great pace, and we quickly came to the Sansiahs' tents.

To give the miserable hovels the dignity of calling them tents is an exaggeration, though this is the meaning of the word "dera" which they call their tents or huts. There was a collection of about fifty of these, and the inhabitants must have numbered about two hundred, men, women and children. The huts were made of reeds reinforced by mud, and were erected all over the place without lay-out, each family having its own hut or set of huts.

By the time we reached the huts, the men of the gang had spotted us coming, and in a vague way, must have realised that something was up. But they had not, of course, realised the significance of the dog. Meanwhile the sub-inspector had brought up the villagers and cut off the retreat of the Sansiahs. On seeing them, the Sansiahs must have realised that it was a police raid.

Actually they had no time to take any steps before the drama of the dog and his working started. I had taken over his chain again by now, and as we came up the hill towards the huts, he pulled me first to one side, then the other. Then suddenly, when we got to the top, he dragged me up to a Sansiah man of about thirty years of age, and made a spring at him. This man leapt off in terror and ran off into one of the huts.

Inquiry showed that he was the owner of the ragged shirt left behind at the scene of the dacoity. There was thus clear evidence that this was the gang responsible for the crime.

The whole tribe was now thoroughly cowed, and first the owner of the shirt, and then another, admitted that they had committed the dacoity. But all this was of no avail to prove the case against them in view of the difficulty already mentioned, that statements to us police officers could not be used in court. We wanted other corroborative evidence, and in particular, wanted to get hold of that part of the stolen property which was identifiable. The Sansiahs had been fly enough not to let on about the property which they had brought and where they had hidden it.

We thought of the idea of casting around the camp with the dog, and as luck would have it, he again got on the trail, which was, of course, still fresh. At one point, as we let him go round, he showed evident signs of interest, and led us off on a trail leading away from the huts. He took us to a well out in the fields which had a good deal of old stone masonry around it, and very soon we found that part of the stonework had recently been tampered with. Further examination revealed a sort of niche in which we found, to our delight, ornaments and trinkets which corresponded with those stolen in the dacoity. Indeed they were subsequently identified by the owners.

With this success we were well content, and I proceeded to leave the encampment with Horatio and his keeper, on the long walk back to the bungalow. I left the sub-inspector behind to arrange for the arrest of all the accused and their conveyance to the District Jail.

We had only gone about five hundred yards before there arose a great uproar in the camp behind us. I hastened back to find that a tragedy had occurred. One of the Sansiah women had deliberately dashed her child's head against a rock, and immediately charged the sub-inspector with having hit the child with his stick. Immediate inquiry quickly served to show that the woman had killed her own child in order to entangle the police officer, and thus throw doubt on the whole proceedings of arrest for the dacoity.

It is impossible to describe the low state of mind and morals of these wandering criminal tribes and they, particularly their women-folk, will not stick at any act, however degrading and disgusting, if they think it will serve their purpose. In this case, undoubtedly my return to the scene and the holding of an immediate inquiry, saved the sub-inspector from having to face a serious charge.

Of course this vile act reacted on the Sansiah woman who was duly convicted of murder. Nor did it, in any way, affect the position as regards the guilt of the men accused in the dacoity case, or distract from the sensation which the work of the dog, Horatio, caused in the district, particularly among the criminal community. The success achieved served to put a stop temporarily to heinous crime in the district.

This unexpected success taught us many things about the science of dog tracking – and in particular showed what a physical ordeal was involved for dogs and man. This run had been over about fifteen miles, and only our frequent rests saved both dogs and men from conking out. We realised, in particular, that we must always have water with us to refresh the dogs on route. This factor would no doubt not apply so strongly to other breeds of dogs.

As I relate in the next chapter, however, the high degree of success achieved in this and later cases had unfortunate results for Basanta and his charges.

Dog's Work Part II

In the ensuing eighteen months or so we continued to achieve success with the dogs in varying degrees. We secured several convictions in court, largely as a result of corroborative evidence being available, and generally, the case as presented in court did not include any evidence of the fact that it was the tracking by the dogs which led to the cases being solved. In one remarkable case, however, we had no other course but to include evidence as to how we got on to the track of the murderer.

One night I had decided to go round the city to check on the patrolling by the city police staff in various localities. Indian cities were very congested, and in the days before the advent of Improvement Trusts and Development Boards they were even more so. The streets dividing lines of houses were often mere lanes in which it would have been impossible to take a vehicle of any sort. There were very few open spaces and the houses mostly adjoined each other with no intervening gardens, etc. The lighting in the streets was from oil lamps, put up few and far between. After ten o'clock, or in the winter much earlier, there were practically no wayfarers in the streets, though in the hot weather, a large number of the poorer classes placed their beds in the streets and slept there. These beds were made of light wood and string, and were easily carried about. To be found moving about the streets at night was, in itself, a suspicious circumstance, and explanations had to be offered to the patrolling police who were not easily satisfied without carrying you off to the police station.

The night of this affair was in the cold weather and there was hardly a human being to be seen. The city seemed to be given up to stray dogs (the ubiquitous pi-dog) and innumerable cattle whom the owners had let out from their houses to forage for food on the garbage and rubbish of the streets. I and my orderly constable moved about the city, occasionally coming across police patrols, and in one instance stumbling upon a whole patrol asleep in the verandah of shop! Suitable retribution overtook the delinquents next day in the orderly room!

At one place, however, we came across something far more serious, a stark murder in fact. Out of what was later ascertained to be an old coach-house, there came a trickle of blood flowing across the street, I happened to pick it up in the light of the Bull's Eye Lantern which I carried. Of course we stopped to investigate. On opening the huge door of the coach-house we found a charpoy, and on it was lying a young woman of about nineteen years of age. Her throat had been cut and she was quite dead. There was no one else in the room in which a small oil-lamp was still burning.

The girl had evidently been murdered without being able to call for help and there was no eye-witness. None of the neighbours admitted having heard a sound or a cry and no one would say who the girl was. It was clearly a crime of passion, though the girl seemed to be a cut above the ordinary prostitute. The murder could only have been committed a short time before our arrival. The body was still warm. It looked as if the murderer had left no trace or clue. He had walked about the room in bare feet, but there were no footprints outside, and he must have put his shoes on before departing. Besides the bedding on the charpoy and the clothes on the girl's body, there was nothing immediately visible, but a search of the bedding disclosed a "kulla". This was a sort of cap worn mostly by Muhammedans inside the turban to keep it in position on the head. Otherwise there was no clue to go on at all. I wasted no time, therefore, and hastened off back to the bungalow to get one of the dogs, leaving my orderly with strict injunctions not to allow anyone, even the local police, to come near the body, or even near the coach-house.

I brought back Belinda with me because she had shown more aptitude for town work than Horatio, and there was no likelihood of any great physical strain being involved. I went to the police station on my way back and took with me to the scene of the occurrence, the sub-inspector in charge and some constables.

In spite of having been woken from her night's sleep and it being well past midnight, Belinda was only too keen for the job in hand. Basanta, her handler, had great difficulty in restraining her. I suppose the scent from the Kulla and the recent footprints was so strong that the dog was just saying to us, "What are you wasting time for? Let me get on with it and I will soon show you your man".

When we did start off, a party of six of us, we had to go the whole way at a run, much to the discomfort of the corpulent sub-inspector who brought up the rear of the party at some considerable distance. The dog took us through various lanes and by-ways for about a mile through the city, till we came to the Ganges canal which flowed at one side of it. There we came to a 'dharmsala' – a place where travellers put up – in fact a sort of hotel (though no food is served and the institution is generally under the management of some charitable organisation). The main door of the dharmsala was shut but not bolted and it took some time to open it. This was fortunate as the delay allowed the sub-inspector to catch us up.

When at length, we managed to open the door, Belinda pushed on inside the courtyard and straight on into one of the rooms, which was found to be occupied by a young Frontier Pathan about twenty-two years of age. This man was sitting on a charpoy in the room. Belinda went in and put her paws on his shoulders. His reaction was remarkable. On seeing the dog and the police party (we were all in uniform), he said in Pushtu: "The day of my wedding has come", a Pushtu proverb meaning "It's all up with me". By good luck the sub-inspector was also a Pathan and knew Pushtu, so understood what the man meant.

The young man was immediately arrested and made a full confession admitting, in particular, to the ownership of the kulla (which was missing from his turban). He had had a row with the girl with whom he had been carrying on for some time because she was allowing other young men to visit her. After committing the murder he had first come back to the dharmsala and changed those of his clothes which had got blood-stained. These clothes he had tied up with stones and thrown them into the canal, from where the police duly retrieved them the next day, after several hours of diving and dredging operations.

The case against the young Pathan was clear. After the investigation had been completed he was sent for trial. The trial became a *cause célèbre* because of the important legal points it raised, first in the Sessions Court and later, on appeal to the High Court.

In the Sessions Court, the point raised was whether the statement made in Pushtu by the accused could be brought on the record. Admittedly his subsequent detailed confession could not, as he retracted it. We could only bring evidence to that part of the statement which led us to drag the canal and recover the blood-stained clothes. The prosecution contended that the remark, in a foreign tongue, would not have been recognised as a confession or an admission, but for the presence of the Pushtu-knowing sub-inspector. It was a statement made by the accused, not to a police officer, but a spontaneous utterance made because of the sudden action of the dog and the arrival of the police party. The defence argued that the presence of a Pushtu-knowing officer had the effect of making the utterance a confession which should be ruled as inadmissible – to which the prosecution countered that the accused could not possibly have known that the subinspector understood Pushtu. In the result, the Sessions Judge convicted the accused and sentenced him to death, but he was not hanged.

In the High Court, a different point was taken by the barrister who was engaged for the defence. This gentleman was, at the time, nearing the peak of his distinguished career, and was recognised as the finest criminal lawyer in India. He put his point somewhat as follows:

> *Milord, I cannot but congratulate the police on the promptness and skill with which they tackled and worked out this case, but I would submit that Your Lordship has no other course but to accept this appeal. It is accepted as legal axiom that if there exists any element of doubt, at least of reasonable doubt, the benefit must be given to the accused. I submit, Milord, that in*

spite of its seeming completeness, this case has an aspect which raises a very serious doubt. Further, I would say that, but for the fact that a senior police officer was directly engaged in the enquiry, the circumstances might have reflected very seriously on the bona fides of the police action.

Milord, this case rests solely on the action of a dumb animal, a dog. We are told that this dog pursued a certain line of action and went over a particular route through the city from which the police came to the conclusion that the accused was the murderer. But how are we to be sure of the reasons which actuated the dog to take this line of action and to follow this particular route? We cannot ask the dog to explain. The dog cannot be produced in court and put up for cross-examination, and consequently we are left to guess at her reasons.

Milord, we know that police officers are fully acquainted with night life of the city and all the sordid sexual intrigues that go on. We may take it for granted that they were fully cognisant of the misconduct of the deceased and of the identity of her paramours. Possibly even some of the young men of the Force were on the list. Is it not possible that, in order to shield the real offender, and at least at the instance of one of these paramours, the police have ingeniously fastened the crime on to this innocent youth? Do we really know that it was the accused's trail that the dog followed? Can we be sure that while their officer was away getting the dog, somebody did not suborn the police to make a trail to the dharmsala where the accused was staying? And may not the dog have been following a faked trail? Is it not possible that the wily and experienced sub-inspector took advantage of the inexperience of his officer, a junior man, to play up to his well known keenness to show the excellence of the blood-hound?

At least, Milord, there is a strong element of doubt in the case. We cannot put the alternative to the dog. I ask Your Lordship not to admit as relevant the statement made by the accused in Pushtu. In view of the doubt in the case, my client is entitled to an acquittal.

This brilliant defence was accepted and the accused was acquitted. How easily are the scales of justice tilted!

This finding had a serious effect on the manner in which evidence about the action of the dogs was presented and accepted in subsequent cases, and our style was very seriously cramped as a result. But it was unfortunate further happenings which put an end to our activities in using dogs as detection aids. Before detailing these, I cannot refrain from repeating a story concerning the barrister who brought about the acquittal of the murderer.

This far-famed lawyer was very diminutive in stature. On one occasion a heated legal discussion arose in court and the opposing legal luminary lost his temper. He turned to the Bench and said:

"Milord, I must protest against the bullying and hectoring attitude adopted by the learned counsel for the plaintiff. Why! He is so small that I could pick him up with one hand and put him in my pocket."

"In that case, Milord, said the diminutive barrister, "my friend would have more brains in his pocket than in his head"!

But to revert to the dogs, such a fear had sprung up among the criminal fraternity of the capabilities of these dogs that certain elements among them determined to get rid of the dogs. As we learned later, the first step they took was to approach Basanta to accept a bribe and poison the dogs or allow them to be poisoned. Unfortunately, although he resolutely refused to betray his loyalty or have anything to do with this project, he did not give us any information of this conspiracy, and the dogs continued to live without adequate protection. One evening, as he was exercising the two in a sort of public park where there were actually but few visitors, a gang of ruffians, about fifteen in number, set on Basanta and the dogs and, in a most cruel manner, belaboured them to death.

This dastardly deed was abhorred by all public-spirited persons and, not least, by the members of the police force, who left no stone unturned to discover the identity of the murderers and bring them to justice. A number of the gang were caught and convicted, the three ringleaders being condemned to death.

It was a sad end to the careers of Horatio and Belinda. Graves were dug for them in the Police Lines and memorial stones erected over them. As we had enlisted Basanta as a constable, his wife and family were given pensions, albeit somewhat meagre, but a public collection was organised for them and this materially eased their position.

By this time the First World War was in full swing and we were never able to replace the murdered dogs. Nor was I ever able to pursue the theory and practice of the use of dogs for police work. But Horatio and Belinda had fully proved their worth and value, though handled in an amateurish and unskilled way.

A Trio of Incidents

To depict the variety which marked the life of a District Officer in the Indian services would take volumes. The following trio of incidents which occurred on successive days, or rather nights, gives some idea of the varied situations experienced by these officers. I, as a police officer, had my fair share.

It was in that "middle" period of the year in India between the end of the hot weather and the rains, and the beginning of the cold weather. It corresponds roughly with our English autumn. At this period you felt that the discomforts and rigours of the hot weather were behind you – memories shortly to be swallowed up in the enjoyment of the Indian winter, when, at least in the United Provinces, the land is blessed with the best climate in the world.

This trio of incidents started on a Sunday when my wife and I had gone out by car in the evening to see whether there were any signs of duck and snipe having come in, after their summer migration to cooler climes. Also with us was a young officer who had joined my staff from the Provincial Police Training College. Our journey back to our bungalow lay through the centre of the city which had become cinema land. Three cinema halls had been put up recently in this area; not the Palaces of the European type, but nevertheless they were fast becoming the big attraction to a large part of the city's population, particularly of the underworld, and its hooligan element. Its potential as a trouble centre had not yet been appreciated and preventive police measures were meagre. This has, of course, since been remedied, but in those early days of the cinema it was left to the beat constables to maintain law and order outside these places.

On this particular evening, two rival bands of hooligans – one

Hindu and the other Muslim – had, by accident or design, clashed outside these cinemas. By the time we arrived on the scene a pretty hot riot had started, and endeavouring to restore order were but two constables. Their efforts were naturally unsuccessful and the hooligans took little heed of them. As for us, our car reached the spot before we realised that there was trouble, while, in the ill-lighted area, the hooligans had not noticed our arrival. On seeing the fight, I realised that this was a communal affair which, if allowed to continue, would set light to communal fires throughout the whole city. I hastily made up my mind to go into the fray with the two orderlies who were with me. I told my assistant to stay in the car with my wife, and though armed only with light canes, we set upon the struggling hooligans and took them completely by surprise. Both sides in the struggle thought that police reinforcements in force had arrived, and did not realise that these reinforcements consisted of but three of us. There was a cry of "polis agai" (the police have come) – and the rioters scattered and fled, leaving four of their number in our hands. Surprise and avoirdupois had worked. The young assistant, who weighed about ten stone (I was nearly double that weight), turned to my wife and said, "Yes I see how its done, but what do men of my size do in a show like that"?

Having made the necessary arrangements for preventing any further trouble, we resumed our homeward journey.

The next day, the second incident took place. About midnight the telephone bell started to ring, and I found someone calling me from the Sadr Bazaar area. That part of the town was in the jurisdiction of the military authorities and was inhabited by camp followers and other people whose occupation was connected with the presence of the military. The speaker was a local lawyer, and he said, "Sahib, come along quickly, the British soldiers are shooting and killing us".

As it was past midnight, I could scarce credit this statement, but I then reflected that these were the days of the celebration of the Ram Lila or Dasehra festivals. Then, in various parts of the city, episodes of the festival were being depicted in plays on temporary stages, and worship also took place at the temples through the night. I could not conceive what could have happened to warrant any shooting, still less shooting by British soldiers. So I decided to go along myself. I woke up a couple of orderlies and we got out the car and went off.

On the way we actually heard two or three stray rifle shots. When we got to the lawyer's house in the Sadr Bazaar, I found that a crowd had collected to worship in the near-by temple. At the moment they were all taking cover in the neighbouring houses. I was shown the bodies of three men who had been shot dead. I was also shown how three bullets had gone clean through the idol in the middle of the temple, a fact that was worrying and incensing the crowd even more than the human casualties. The extraordinary thing was that these bullets had passed harmlessly through the midst of a crowd of about one hundred persons seated on the ground in front of the idol, but the three men who had been standing on the ground outside the temple did not escape.

The shots had been fired from rising ground about sixty yards off, and even as I peered round (it was full moonlight) I could see a figure silhouetted against the sky on the top of the mound. It was a British soldier in uniform and he was carrying a rifle. I tried to get near him and was making my way up the mound when he turned and disappeared down the other side.

It was clear that the soldier must be a man from one of the military guards; otherwise he would not be able to get hold of a rifle and ammunition. It was almost certainly one who had left his sentry post. I accordingly went round the various units and found all the sentries present, except at the last unit some distance away from the Sadr Bazaar. Here all was quiet, and I was not challenged as I approached the guardroom. I managed to wake up the N.C.O. in charge and asked him where his sentry was. He naturally thought he must be on duty and said so in no polite terms. However, he at length came out with me to look, and when we got to the sentry-box there was no sentry, but, significantly, six empty beer bottles!

The N.C.O. turned out the whole guard and a search was made. We went to the bed of the missing man in his barrack away from the guardroom. He was not there but he had evidently been there, for his bandolier was thrown on the bed. There were twenty rounds missing. On further search in the vicinity of the Sadr Bazaar, we came upon him lying in a ditch, still grasping his rifle. Two of us leapt upon him and after a tussle – drink gave him extra strength, as it often does – we overpowered him. A live bullet was still in the barrel of his rifle!

Later he came to his senses, and recovered from the stupor which had been brought on by the beer. The poor fellow had genuinely no recollection of what he had done. When told he had caused the death of three persons he was terribly shocked.

The case against him was clear but there was a good deal of discussion of his responsibility in law for his actions. Intoxication is no defence unless it can be proved that the liquor was unwillingly or unknowingly taken. In this case there could be no such suggestion. Fortunately for the young soldier there was a medical history behind him which indicated an epileptic past. Obviously it was not serious or he would have been invalided out of the Army, but the evidence of this medical history produced by the defence was sufficient to sway the jury and the judge. He was acquitted but remanded to a mental home to come up for judgement in the indefinite future.

During the period of his trial, when the discussions were going on out of court as to his legal liability, he was kept in civil custody in a special lock-up for Europeans. In order to give him exercise, he was allowed to play games with my police recruits. He made himself popular with these lads by his athletic prowess and simple manners. He took up learning the language and, in the ten weeks he was in our custody, he became quite proficient. It was a sad comment on the havoc caused by the Demon Drink to an apparently normal young man of intelligence and promise.

The third incident of the trio also took place at night. Again, well after midnight, the telephone bell rang. A voice said, "Sahib come quickly and help us". "What's wrong", I said. The voice replied, "a crocodile is holding up the main street". Once again I could not credit the news. The place referred to was a suburb of the city, about six miles from the area where I lived, and was, incidentally, fully a mile from the riverside. How did a crocodile come to get in such a place? However I got up, dressed and proceeded forth in my car, armed with a .280 Ross rifle. By the time I got there, in spite of the time of night, a large crowd had collected. The animal had by now got into a private compound, and into an outhouse used as a kitchen. A woman was actually cooking there at the time. On seeing the crocodile, she became petrified with fright and was crouched in the corner of the room, too afraid to move. The crocodile was lying along the other side, swinging its tail in a truly alarming way. When I managed to get a look in at the room, the woman would not budge. A bullet would possibly ricochet off its body on to the woman. To get a vital shot in a manner not likely to ricochet, I had to get on to the roof of the building, have a hole cut in it, and then let down a lantern, and shoot the animal from above. Actually this was an easy operation, and the animal was duly shot – but its tail continued to lash alarmingly in its death convulsions for some time. Eventually this movement ceased, and we dragged the dead animal out. I returned home with a ten foot crocodile tied on to the back of my car. It somehow or other got laid up in a creek far away from the main stream, and when the waters subsided after the rains, it must have found itself high and dry. It was proceeding, no doubt, to make its way to the river but in doing so, had to go through a considerable area of habitation, and thus it met its fate. I very much doubt whether a crocodile had ever been shot in such a place, and in such conditions, at dead of night.

But this trio of incidents was typical of the experiences of officers who served India in the various Services.

Sher Singh Dacoit Leader

The life of a successful dacoit is generally short but merry. Sher Singh was the exception that proved the rule. In spite of the fact that he was eventually captured alive and sent for trial for innumerable dacoities and murders, he spent only two years in jail and became a prosperous corn chandler.

His father was a successful village farmer, but after his father's death he became extravagant and a leader of the local youths. In order to gratify his desires, he turned to a life of crime – burglary, cattle theft and, finally, dacoity. Any robbery committed by five or more persons was legally termed dacoity. He initially joined a readymade gang but soon became the leader.

Initial successes made the gang bolder and they became a perfect terror to the countryside. Of course they came in conflict with the police and their identity became known. They had to leave their houses and become outlaws. This in its turn meant that they had to commit more crime to live, but their planning became more difficult as the police were hunting them. On the other hand they had succeeded in obtaining more firearms, guns, pistols and a rifle or two. They were able to attack more wealthy persons, ensconced in stronger and less accessible houses. Their fame and reputation grew and they had no lack of youths wanting to join them. So great a name had Sher Singh acquired that he became a regular bogie in the neighbourhood. Mothers used to silence their crying children by saying to them, "Hush! If you don't keep quiet, Sher Singh will come and get you".

The gang must have committed more than one hundred dacoities and the leaders took to hiring themselves out as assassins to bump off the enemies of any person who was willing to pay them enough.

But they had to keep on changing their headquarters and often to spend their time in the fields or in the Jungle. They were in constant dread of being given away to the police. At the same time the police were finding the greatest difficulty in getting trace of their exact whereabouts. People were scared stiff of giving us any information; nevertheless we managed to get to know of their presence at various places in sufficient time and with sufficient accuracy to enable us to make raids. We found, however, that the birds had flown on every occasion and we were at a loss to understand how the gang had got to know that we had actually started out after them. We were to discover the reason for that later.

Meanwhile rewards for the capture of Sher Singh were notified at the unheard of amount of Rs 10,000. It was probably the size of the reward which led one of his gang to give him away. Sher Singh and his gang had long been planning to raid the house of a minor Raja who was known to possess a veritable battery of guns and rifles which his father had acquired for sport. The present Raja was known to be a pusillanimous person who would probably surrender the arms if only the gang could effect an entry into his fortified house. In the gang was one Bishen Singh who lived in a village close to that of the Raja whose house was right among the ravines. The father of Bishen Singh used to be employed in the garhi (fortified house) and thus Bishen Singh was able to contact the Raja. He knew the topography of the house and could be most useful to Sher Singh in arranging an entry. So Bishen Singh knew all about the projected dacoity to be committed on the Raja's house. The lure of the big reward induced him to plan to give Sher Singh away. He first pointed out to Sher Singh that the gang could safely hide in the Jungles of the ravines round about, and accordingly, just prior to the intended day of attack, the gang made their hideout in these Jungles.

Bishen Singh then invited Sher Singh and his brother outlaws to a feast in his village. He pointed out, however, that it might be dangerous for them to come to his house, but there was an old building which was used as the village school. The school was closed for the vacation and there would be no interruption. It was accordingly arranged that the gang should come to this building until darkness fell, and then they could get back to their hide-out in the ravines. Meanwhile they could have a good sleep in the school building where Bishen Singh had laid out some straw on the floor of the main room.

Having managed to get Sher Singh to agree to all this, Bishen Singh sneaked away in the evening to the camp of a Magistrate who was on tour not far off. The Magistrate immediately brought him to Headquarters by car and took him to my bungalow. Bishen Singh then related how the gang were to be lured to the school building next day and suggested that we should attempt a raid on them while the gang was sleeping in the school. He explained how we could get to a point about a mile from the school where he would meet us. Meanwhile he must get back to his village so that the gang would not come to know of his absence during the night.

So Bishen Singh went off home at once, and the next day the Magistrate and I, with a force of police, set off in two lorries. We could not take these anywhere near the village so had to leave them and walk about four miles through the sweltering heat. The crops were all down and there was no cover, but we managed to get across the open country to the point where Bishen Singh had promised to meet us: a mango grove about a mile from the village. Sure enough he was there, true to his word.

"It is all right Sahib", he said, "Sher Singh is there in the school asleep with nine or ten of his gang. I have locked the door of the school from the outside and Sher Singh himself had insisted on all the window shutters being closed in case some villagers should peer in and see them."

He volunteered this information but was clearly in a great funk. I said to him, "You have done your job splendidly. Now come along and open the door when we have surrounded the place".

No Sahib, I daren't do that. If it should by any chance become known to Sher Singh that I had given him away, my life would be in great danger. I will give you the key but I won't go a step further with you".

Although this made me doubt whether, after all, he had not brought us on a wild goose chase and was preparing to make himself scarce as soon as we discovered it, there was nothing for it but to go on with the raid. We might find the gang was not there at all, or at least that they were on the alert and might effect their escape before we could surround them. So after giving the men a short rest we proceeded forward stealthily to approach the school. We had practised the manoeuvre entailed in surrounding a place like this quietly and quickly, so we had no difficulty in putting it into operation once again. Owing, however, to the lack of cover, the whole line, in the form of a pair of pincers, had to crawl along on the ground till each man reached his position, and the pincers joined up. The operation was performed with success without the party in the school (if, indeed, they were there) becoming aware of our presence. Some of the men were then told to climb on to the roof of the building as soon as I opened the door. I intended to open the door, and relying on superior numbers, to summon the gang to surrender.

The surrounding operation being complete, I crept forward to the door. The unlocking proved to be a somewhat difficult and noisy operation, but it was done eventually, and I crept in only to find myself in a sort of small entrance hall with another door in front leading to the main room. It was pitch dark, but I did not want to use the torch I carried with me till I had got through the second door. I crept stealthily on and opened this second door. I stood up with the intention of challenging the gang, thinking they were still asleep. Unfortunately they had been awakened by the noise of my unlocking the first door. As I entered through the second door, one of them, who had evidently awakened first and had been waiting behind the door, let fly with a sword. By great good fortune, I was wearing a pith sunhat or helmet. The ceiling was not very high and he could not get in a full length blow. He crushed my helmet but I escaped with a minor head injury. This afterwards gave me a lot of trouble as it went sceptic owing to the sword being covered with rust.

I immediately emptied my automatic pistol into the room which was in pitch darkness. Some of the gang also let off with their guns.

I beat a hasty retreat through yet a third door which led straight into the open courtyard. I knew then that we had got them trapped and that Bishen Singh, in spite of his funk, had not let us down.

Meanwhile the gang could not see outside the building or realise that they were surrounded as they themselves had got the windows shuttered up, nor did they know whether there was anyone on the roof. They thought they could effect their escape by climbing the inside staircase onto the roof. Unfortunately for them one of my havildars was there, just by the opening where the staircase led onto the roof, and as the first man came up into the opening, he shot him. This man fell back onto the staircase, and naturally the gang also came to a halt. My havildar shouted exultantly, "I have killed the great Sher Singh".

While this was happening I had come out into the open and was looking round the building to see what could be done. Some of my officers and men had heard the firing and had, unknown to me, rushed into the building through the first door. Creeping round the building, I had found an opening in one of the window shutters; I peered in and saw a clump of men in the main room whom I took to be the gang. I was just going to empty my pistol again at them when I saw a glint of a uniform button, and realised just in time that I was about to fire on my own men. I was rather shattered at the thought of the dreadful mistake which I so nearly made.

It was still pitch dark in the main room from which the gang had already, as we have seen, moved out. I saw we must get light into the room and called up some men to tear down the wooden window shutters. I then joined those of our party who had got into the building, and we pressed forward to the door at the end of the main room which led to the staircase. On seeing us, the gang who had come headlong down the staircase, tried to slam the door, but 1 managed to seize hold of the arm of the first man, who thus got jammed in the doorway. I pulled on the arm and the others pulled on me and the owner of the arm was thus forced through the door. It was none other than Sher Singh himself (not shot dead, as my havildar had claimed). He struggled manfully but was, of course, soon overpowered.

The rest of the gang then gave in and were duly captured, all nine of them. When they had been secured I passed through the far door onto the staircase where I found a body lying on the stairs face downwards. I turned the body over and was astonished to find that he was Jagannath Singh, an armed police constable of the last district I had been in, where he had been one of my personal orderlies! I now understood why we had drawn blank in our previous raids and how the gang came to know of our movements. This man had taken six months' leave from his district and had joined Sher Singh's gang. He was, in fact, a resident of this district, and it was made his job to spy on the police at Headquarters and give timely warning to the gang of any sign of a police party leaving Headquarters. I came to know that he had actually visited some pals in our Reserve Police Lines three days before our raid, but so successfully had Bishen Singh hidden his own movements and so quickly had we been able to act this time, that Jagannath Singh did not come to know of the raid and thus the gang got no warning this time. Jagannath Singh must have only just rejoined the gang when we arrived.

Sher Singh and his men were handcuffed and brought in triumph to Headquarters where they were lodged in the District Jail. The order required a medical examination, by the Jail doctor, of all persons brought into the jail. On examining Sher Singh, the doctor found a bullet wound in his face. One of my .32 pistol bullets had entered his face and lodged in his nose, whence it was extracted. It must have ricocheted off the wall or floor of the room – otherwise the wound would have been more serious. Nevertheless it must have been very painful, yet Sher Singh had never uttered a word or complained at all of being wounded. I had noticed his face was smeared with blood, but assumed he had got some scratches in the scuffle. He was a tough 'un that Sher Singh, and he lived up to his name ('sher' is a lion) to the end.

His luck now seemed to have deserted him and his future looked black. He seemed booked for the gallows but it turned out that his luck still held. The money which he had earned as an outlaw now stood him in good stead, and was spent freely on his behalf. He was sent up for trial on the maximum number of cases allowed, but such a terror had his name inspired that many witnesses were afraid to give evidence. Money was spent not only in suborning those who did give evidence, but also in bribing minor police and court officials. In the result, after trials lasting more than two years, Sher Singh was acquitted, either originally or on appeal, in all cases of murder and dacoity. He was convicted and sentenced to two years imprisonment for illegal possession of arms. As we did not want to produce Bishen Singh as a witness (in which case his life would not have been worth a week's purchase), we could not prove that the gang had collected on this occasion to commit a dacoity on the Raja's house. This would in itself have led to a conviction earning seven years' imprisonment. Sher Singh was even acquitted in the case of murder for which his two brothers had been convicted and hanged (they had been caught earlier on in the campaign). The chief witness in that case had since died and the High Court held that there was insufficient evidence against Sher Singh without the verbal deposition of this witness. So his luck held, and after two years he came out of jail. He did not return to his village home but, out of his remaining ill-gotten gains, he set up a grain dealing business in Headquarters.

After his release, when I happened to revisit the district, I met him in the town and we discussed, in a friendly way, the details of the campaign against him, in particular, the events leading up to his capture.

"That dog Jagannath Singh got his deserts. I always thought I was making a great mistake in taking a policeman into my gang, although he was the brother of my most trusted lieutenant. My first thoughts turned out to be correct. I realise now that you must have put him into my gang and that it was he who brought you along to Bishen Singh's village. Otherwise no one else would have dared to give us away".

"Quite right, you old scoundrel" I said.

For I was content to let him think that it was the dead Jagganath Singh who had betrayed him. Had I disillusioned him of his belief, it would not have been long before he would have taken revenge on Bishen Singh, in spite of his having ostensibly turned over a new leaf and decided to lead an honest life.

A Tale of Two Heads

The first part of this story deals with a body without a head; the second part is about a head without a body.

One day at a big railway station in India, a carriage cleaner found a trunk which had been left in a compartment of a train standing at a siding. An offensive smell was emanating from it so the cleaner went and made a report at the railway police station. The police duly made an inspection and found that the trunk contained a man's headless body. The body was wrapped in a sort of shirt, otherwise there were no clothes or any other article in the box. There was no mark of identity on the body and the only thing to go on, in an attempt to establish the identity of the deceased, was a washerman's mark on the shirt. This mark was a circle with two crosses and two dots on it thus: (⁙). Medical examination of the body was made by the Civil Surgeon who considered that it was the body of a Hindu male under thirty years of age. He thought the decapitation had been done after death. There were no signs of poisoning in the stomach. The decapitation had been done by somebody with knowledge of anatomy and with some skill. He suggested that it had been done by a butcher or the like, but he did not exclude the possibility of someone in the medical profession.

The compartment was part of a train which had come up from the Calcutta side, and which had been run into a siding and left there for some hours. This would appear to indicate that the murder must have taken place in some town near the railway line on the Calcutta side.

The local police were obviously not equipped with resources for dealing with the case, so the Chief Constable of the district had asked for the services of a CID officer. The inquiry had clearly to be based initially on an endeavour to trace which dhobi (washerman) used this particular mark. In view of the possible area involved this verily appeared to be a case of looking for a needle in the proverbial haystack. However, we first called in the local dhobis, the majority of whom considered from the mark and the shirt itself, that it had been washed by a dhobi who worked on the riverside, and not in a tank or pond, or in well water or piped water. The mark was not owned by any local dhobi. We decided, therefore, to comb out all the stopping places on the line towards Calcutta, which were near the river. Now, when inquiries came to be made, it was discovered that a similar dhobi mark was used by several dhobis, not a great number, but often by more than one in the same place. Every time the Inspector came across this mark, he had to check up on the dhobi's clientele to find out if anyone whose clothes were so marked, was missing. This proved a laborious task but was nevertheless undertaken. When the Inspector eventually reached an important town four hundred miles from the place where the body was found, he reported to me that he had so far drawn blank, and asked for orders. I accordingly told him not to go any further, and called him back for a conference. My argument to him was on these lines:

"I don't think we need look further than twelve to eighteen hours' run by the particular train in which the body was found. If the murder had taken place at a spot further away, even in this cold weather, the body would have started to emit an offensive smell after about twenty-four hours after the murder. Some time must have elapsed between death and getting the body, after decapitation, into the train. There is no record of anybody in the train noticing a smell from the trunk on the journey. Therefore the journey must have started within, say, eighteen hours or so of the time of the murder. You have checked up in the towns along the railway line far enough to include all the area covered by this period, and you have not come across anyone reported missing of the required age and description. We must start again, and the first thing to do is a more intensive inspection of the scene of the discovery of the body. We must examine the significance of the siding where the train was standing."

Accordingly we journeyed to the railway junction where the quest had started, and made further inquiry about the train in which the body appeared to have been conveyed. The junction was the journey's end for this train, and it was always run into a siding which led away from the main station and across a platform about twenty yards from the main line. On the other side of the siding was the railway fencing that divided the line from the public street that passed along the line. Two possibilities now presented themselves. The trunk could have been placed in the empty compartment at night by some person or persons who could have brought the body from the town and put it over the fence. In this way the trunk might not have travelled by train at all and the murder might have been done locally; or the trunk might, with equal facility, have been brought over the platform at night from some other train.

The Inspector accordingly explored the first possibility. The river Ganges flowed close by, and many of the city dhobis washed clothes on its banks. We had, however, been told that no dhobi of the locality admitted using this mark. There was always the possibility that a dhobi might himself have been the murderer, or an accomplice. Diligent inquiry failed to disprove the dhobis' denial, nor was there any person of the correct age and description reported to be missing. Admittedly the description was itself a matter of guesswork but we knew at least the approximate age and height.

The local inquiry drew a blank, so we decided to explore the other possibility, and here we were helped by a new piece of evidence. A railway coolie (porter) who had been away to his village for some weeks, and had recently returned, now came forward to say that he had been engaged to carry a trunk similar to the one found containing the body, from the main line train coming *from Delhi.* He was instructed to put it near the siding where the train from Calcutta was always drawn up at the end of its journey. He could not say who the passenger was who engaged him, and he doubted his ability to identify him. He did not appear to be a local man.

All this amounted, in one way, to very little in itself, but in another way it was highly significant as it indicated that we had probably been on the wrong track altogether. We had too hastily assumed that the trunk had been carried in the train coming from the Calcutta side. If the coolie's story was correct, we must try in the opposite direction. Fortunately the train now to be considered was a mail train running through from Delhi to Calcutta and it only stopped at a few stations. So there was nothing for it but to repeat the method of inquiry at the stopping places of this train up to Delhi, and even beyond. The Inspector spent a comparatively short time on the intervening stations and duly came to Delhi. There flows the great river Jumna, and hundreds of Delhi dhobis wash clothes on the riverside. He started to comb these out. A week's inquiry found no less than half a dozen dhobis using the sought-after mark. So he had to go through the clientele of all six, and once again no-one appeared to be missing.

Meanwhile the times and distances had been carefully checked again, and we came to the conclusion that Delhi was just about the right distance to be the place where the murder might have been committed. I went along to Delhi myself and met my Inspector. I said to him, "This is our last chance. Unless we find something here we're finished, beaten".

"I agree, Sahib", said the Inspector, "but I don't see what we can do. I can't find another dhobi who uses the mark. We might perhaps go further along the line beyond Delhi".

I then bethought me of the Civil Surgeon's report. It was a veritable brainwave!

"Inspector Sahib", I said, "I somehow do not think that the body would have been brought from beyond Delhi. This would have entailed a change of train, and would have been risky. But just think back to the report of the Civil Surgeon. You remember that he said that he thought that the decapitation had been done by a butcher or a medical man. Why not try this line of thought? Go through the list of clients of your six dhobis and see if there are any butchers or medical men, or anybody likely to have sufficient knowledge of anatomy, to do the beheading skilfully".

So the Inspector started off again. The dhobi's list of customers whose clothes bore this mark produced about twenty persons possibly answering to this description. None of these persons were missing and, of course, the man with anatomic knowledge was not the victim but the murderer, and would therefore not be missing unless he had indeed absconded after the murder. It therefore seemed to be worthwhile to have them all interrogated, and accordingly this was done. Among them was one Dr. Tara Chand who had a general practice in a low and crowded area of Delhi. He had a dispensary in the main bazaar but lived in a house some distance off. He admitted that his clothes were marked with the significant mark but denied ownership of the shirt or any knowledge of the body. After interviewing the doctor, the Inspector reported to me in my hotel, and said:

> "This doctor Tara Chand seemed strangely nervous when I saw him in his dispensary. I think it is likely that I may get something from further inquiries in his direction".

He left straightway and, with the help of the local police, soon came to know of a very sinister fact. The doctor had a wife much younger than himself, and she was reported to be carrying on with a young medical student, who frequently visited the house. His name was Ram Sumer and he was getting some sort of tuition from the doctor. This young man had not been seen about for some months. He was a resident of a distant district of the Punjab, and naturally the neighbours did not worry about his disappearance, having thought he must have gone home.

This item of information seemed highly significant and I decided to interview the doctor myself at his home. So I and the Inspector went along to the house, which was an ordinary dwelling house near a crowded muhalla (city ward), but separated from the rest of the muhalla by an open space and a deep ravine. We found the doctor at home. He had been nervous with the Inspector when he was first interviewed at his dispensary, but when the Inspector left him he must have become reassured. To be again so soon visited by the Inspector, this time in company of a high officer made him all the more nervous. Nevertheless he kept his presence of mind sufficiently to answer our questions as to the whereabouts of his student friend quite reasonably. He said that Ram Sumer had given up his studies and gone to his native home in the Punjab. He must have known this would take some time to verify, and that it was a plausible explanation of the young man's disappearance.

We had been conducting our interrogation of the doctor in a small room in his house, with but very little furniture in it. There were no carpets or any such appendages and it had a mud floor, as do most houses of persons of this status in Indian towns. I noticed a remarkable thing, that he kept on shifting his chair about. I could not account for this activity for some time, but gradually I got to form the idea that there was something more than sheer nervousness to account for this activity with the chair. I started testing the ground near me with my shoe, and I found some indication that the earth of the floor was giving way slightly, and I then noticed that the legs of his chair as he moved about were making an impression on the ground. Had the doctor something to hide? And was it connected with the mud floor? If not, why this apparent anxiety on his part about the floor?

On the pretence of taking notes of his answers to our questions, I scribbled a note to the Inspector, and passed it over to him:

Watch the doctor's antics with his chair. I think it means something. Get along out on some excuse, and bring the local police and some search witnesses. We must investigate the floor further.

The Inspector got up and said:

"Oh Sir, I quite forgot there is a witness whom I had arranged to meet at the police station at this time. If you will excuse me, I will go and question him. and meet you back here in a short while".

"Right, Inspector Sahib", I said, "I have no doubt the doctor and I will be able to while away the time talking about affairs in general. Don't be too long, because I want to get back to make a report to Headquarters. Take my car, of course".

So off went the Inspector, and I engaged the doctor in conversation about various matters. When the Inspector came back, he had with him not only the local police sub-inspector and some constables, but also two respectable persons of the locality, who would act as search witnesses, and most significant of all, a coolie with a spade. As soon as he saw the spade, the doctor must have realised our intention. He asked permission to go out to ease himself.

Suspecting that he intended to abscond, I sent a constable with him. The doctor went into the adjoining room and opened a cupboard, which was the place where he kept his store of medicines. The constable noticed him put something in his mouth, and shortly afterwards he collapsed to the ground. The constable came rushing in to report this, but by the time we got to the doctor he was obviously in a bad way. He had clearly taken some quick-acting poison. In a few minutes he was dead.

In spite of this dramatic and tragic development, we had to go on with the operation for which we had called in the local police. The mud floor of the doctor's sitting-room was dug up, and buried under it, or rather in it, was a human head in a most unsightly state. Although there was not much offensive smell, the head was beyond recognition. It was taken out and sent to the civil Surgeon for examination. His report showed it to be the head of a person of the age given by the earlier examination of the body. Death had been almost certainly caused by a bullet wound at the back of the head.

Further investigation was almost superfluous, but the necessary inquiries were put through. Sufficient evidence was forthcoming to prove conclusively that the head belonged to the body found in the railway compartment some six months previously, and that the head and body were those of the medical student, Ram Sumer. A search of the doctor's house resulted in the finding of a pistol in another room, underneath a pile of clothes. It was of a calibre from which the fatal shot could have been fired, causing the wound in the head.

It was now possible to reconstruct the murder. The doctor must have come to know of his wife's infidelity, and of her intrigue with the young Punjabee. The liaison had been going on for some time before the doctor came to know of it, and he probably lulled the young man into thinking that he had not discovered it. But he had been brooding over the treachery of the youth who had repaid his assistance in this manner, and he had been searching for some means to take his revenge. He probably continued to gain the young man's confidence, and then one day he must have come up behind him, perhaps while he was engaged in study, and shot him in the back of the head. The house was, as we have seen, separated from the neighbouring houses by a ravine, and the shot would not be heard by the neighbours, especially as the pistol was fired behind a closed door.

He had to consider the problem of the disposal of the body. He had worked it all out beforehand. With his medical knowledge he was able to cut off the head, as he had made up his mind to make identification impossible. He treated the head with some chemical which had a preservative effect or, at least, served to eliminate the possibility of smell arising from it, since he had decided to bury it under the floor of his room. I could not fathom the reason for this decision; possibly he argued to himself that this would be the last place anybody would look for it; possibly it was with some sadistic idea of being able to gloat over the success of his revengeful scheme. He then decided to remove the rest of the body as far away as possible. He put it in a trunk and took it to the Railway Station and got into the train with it. Being a medical man he would know how far he could travel with it before it started to stink. He then got out at the railway junction where it was found, and got the trunk deposited on the platform, probably with the idea of just leaving it there. Later the idea must have come to him of putting it into the empty compartment of the train which he found standing in the siding. Whether intentionally or not, it is not possible to say, but this action of his served to delay the fruition of the investigation. As already related, we were put on to the wrong track. He had removed all signs of the deceased's identity and had taken away all the young man's clothes. And then he made his first mistake: he wrapped the body in one of his own shirts, forgetting, no doubt, that it bore a dhobi mark.

Thus was cleared up a mystery which might have remained untraced and unsolved. But the painstaking and patient Inspector was rewarded by seeing his investigation brought to fruition, though the murderer cheated the gallows of another victim by expiating his crime with his own hand. What small things lead to great results in crime investigation! In this case, a Dhobi mark! And how often does a criminal's guilty conscience lead him to give himself away! Had not his guilty conscience impelled him to make his second mistake of shifting his chair about when he was being interrogated, he would probably have got away with it. Even after the discovery of the head, a conviction might have been difficult to obtain, especially as the coolie at the station would probably not have identified him, and all the other evidence was circumstantial.

So much for the body without a head; and now for the head without a body.

Shamaspur was a village lying in a locality well irrigated with canal distributaries and 'minors'. It had a mixed population, among them some tough Jats and Thakurs. These were mostly the servants and labourers of the Old Thakur Surjan Singh, the resident zemindar (landowner) of the village. Several banias (small traders or bankers) lived in the village, and they were not very popular with the other villagers because of their harsh treatment of their debtors.

Among the worst-hated was Bala Din, who was reputed to have fabulous wealth buried in the ground or in the wall of his house. It is not surprising, therefore, that one night he was the victim of a dacoity. A gang of about twenty persons, suddenly at dead of night attacked his house, which was in at one edge of the village. No doubt the dacoits reckoned that no one would come to the aid of the rascally old miser. But they had not reckoned with the proud old zemindar. Men immediately ran to his house and told him of the arrival of the gang in his village. He thought it a great insult that a gang of badmashes (bad characters) should dare to come to his village, and he did not care who their intended victim was. The gang must be opposed, and he immediately ordered his servants to collect a band of villagers to resist the dacoits. The robbers had just succeeded in gaining entrance into the house and seizing the wretched Bala Din, whom they were proceeding to persuade, in no gentle manner, to tell them where he kept his hoard of jewels and cash. If they had been left to themselves they would have, no doubt, soon wrung the information from the cringing banker. Two or three of the gang would be ostentatiously making preparations which clearly indicated an intention to try the effect of a little scorching. Some rags would be dipped in oil, lighted and held in uncomfortable proximity to various tender parts of their victim's body if he was not rapidly forthcoming with the information. Meanwhile others of the gang had kept up much shouting outside to warn off any possible helpers. They also fired a few shots with the same intent, but they only had a small stock of powder and shot, and only muzzle-loading weapons. The leaders thought that there was small chance of the villagers turning out to help the hated bania. Consequently, they were taken completely by surprise when two or three batches of villagers appeared from various directions and attacked them simultaneously, taking no heed of the shouting or even of the shots fired. The dacoits had to beat it after a brisk fight in which several of their number sustained injuries from lathi (stout bamboo stick) blows. One of them was very seriously injured in the head. The dacoits eventually managed to get away in the darkness, dragging their sorely wounded companion with them.

When they got well outside the village they paused to re-assemble and sum up their situation. Their wounded comrade was in a bad way. If they tried to get him away, the villagers, who were probably organising a pursuit, would certainly catch them up, as he would have hindered their escape. They therefore, decided to finish him off themselves. If they just left him, he would almost certainly give them away, so they must kill him. They could not leave the dead body where it was. His identity would be established and this might lead to the identity of the whole gang being disclosed. They decided to cut off his head. They then put his head in the canal 'minor' which flowed by, thinking it would be carried away down stream or sink to the bottom. The body they put in a sack which they had brought to carry off the loot, and hid it in a patch of thick jungle about a half mile off. All these facts were, of course, only ascertained later, and came to light in the manner now related.

Having disposed of their comrade in this manner, the gang dispersed. The villagers had, as a matter of fact, given up the pursuit early on. Some of them went off to the police station about seven miles off. The next morning the local police came in force. and started the investigation. Little was gained by the inspection of the bania's house, as the dacoits had not succeeded in taking away any property, nor even had they time actually to maltreat the inmates. The villagers told the police sub-inspector that there had been a fight and that some of the dacoits (as well as some of the villagers) had been injured, and that the gang had managed to carry off their wounded. So the officer proceeded to make a search of the country round the village, and it was not long before traces of blood were found and unmistakable signs of considerable loss of blood by someone. No wounded person or dead body, however, was found.

Later on, however, the head was found. When they dumped it in the canal 'minor', the dacoits did not know, or had forgotten, that a little down-stream there was a siphon. Unfortunately for them the head got entangled in this. A village boy taking cattle down to drink from the 'minor' came across it. He immediately came and told the sub-inspector and the head was fished out of the siphon. Thus it came about that the head was recovered "in good condition" and perfectly recognisable.

The point was, whose head was it? The news of the dacoity had, of course, immediately been passed on to all neighbouring police stations, as had also the fact that some of the dacoits had been injured. In the village Silehra, in a neighbouring police circle, lived one Gulab, a Chamar by caste. He had been in the dacoity and had been seriously injured, but managed to reach his home. The Mukhia (headman) of his village soon got to know of his injury and sent word to the police. The sub-Inspector of that police circle came along and arrested the wounded man and took a statement from him. While admitting having taken part in the dacoity, he gave the names of a number of persons who, he said, had also taken part, including some well known outlaws. He said that the man who had been decapitated was one Bhupat Ram, by caste a Bania, of Baripur, a village across the Ganges river, about sixty miles off. A copy of this statement was duly sent to the investigating police officer at the village where the crime had occurred.

In the meanwhile a report of the dacoity, which is always sent to the district Chief of Police, wheresoever he may be, was brought out to me on tour. I was moving camp in any case on that day, so I decided to motor over and inspect the scene of the occurrence and see how the inquiry was going. When I started I knew nothing about the developments of the finding of the head or of the confession of the arrested dacoit. I only learnt of these when, accompanied by my wife, I arrived at the village some forty-eight hours after the report of the dacoity at the police station. The head had been recovered by then. It appears that Gulab Chamar had not known of the recovery when he made his statement, otherwise he would not have risked giving a wrong name, if he had known that identification was possible.

On reading the copy of his statement and thinking it rather remarkable that a man by caste a bania should be in a dacoity, I decided to motor across to Baripur village, where the deceased dacoit was said to reside. I took the head in the back of my car in spite of my wife's protests. I promised to do the journey as quickly as possible, but all the time I was being urged to go faster: the head was beginning to get 'high'! On arrival at Baripur I sent for the mukhia and chaukidar (village policeman) and asked if they had heard of the death of Bhupat Ram, Bania; if indeed. such a person resided in the village.

"Bhupat Ram", said the mukhia, "Yes, he lives in my village all right, but he is very much alive. I saw him in the village this morning."

"But I have got his head here in the back of my car. Come and see it for yourself."

So he and the chaukidar came to the car and I showed them the head.

"That's not Bhupat Ram", they both shouted.

"If that is so", said I, "produce Bhupat Ram". And sure enough they went away and brought Bhupat Ram who was found ploughing his field. A fine young fellow he was, and although a Bania by caste, he did not carry on the traditional occupation of trade or banking. Gulab of Silehra had clearly been lying and I had come on a false track.

So I went back to my headquarters, taking the head with me. I took it to the Civil Surgeon.

"Doctor", I said, "inspect this head, and tell us what you make of it. But in any case you must arrange to keep it in an identifiable condition for a month or two".

"That is easy", he said, "I will keep it in spirits".

And he did. He put it in a glass case and kept it under lock and key in the Civil Hospital. He reported later that the head had been decapitated in a brutal and unskilled manner by some sort of instrument such as a hatchet. So we resumed the search for the owner, or rather late owner, of the head. Gulab Chamar, when faced with proof that Bhupat Ram was alive, admitted that he had been induced to give this name by the mukhia of his village who had a quarrel over debts with the family of Bhupat Ram. Not realising that the head would turn up, the mukhia had got this man's name included by Gulab merely to give trouble to the Baripur Bania family. He knew that if the police of the circle were told of the alleged complicity of Bhupat Ram in the dacoity, they would apply pressure to the family. Such is the psychology of the villager, that he would probably abscond in fear and remain away from his home, although the obvious way to disprove the charge would have been simply to prove his continued existence by turning up at the police station. The Silehra mukhia had not bargained for my interference and the prompt testing of Gulab's confession which led to the quick disclosure of the falsity of the charge against Bhupat Ram. He was thus not only cheated of his revenge against his enemies in Baripur, but he lost his job as mukhia and went to jail for trying to fabricate false evidence.

Some days passed before any further development, but at the monthly parade of village policemen, held at yet a third police station, one of the chaukidars did not turn up. No report had been received from his village to account for his absence. Accordingly inquiries were made and it was found that he had not been seen since the night of the dacoity. The idea was formed that possibly he had been in the dacoity. His wife was brought into Headquarters and when shown the head, identified it as that of her late husband. Asked why she had not told anybody about his absence, she replied she had told the mukhia of the village. It was then found that the mukhia himself had formed a gang, and it was his gang which had committed the dacoity. The chaukidar was a member of the gang. It was small wonder that the absence of the chaukidar had not been reported at the police station.

The mukhia was also duly arrested. Meanwhile, Gulab Chamar, who had been under treatment in the district hospital and also under arrest, was again interrogated, and was induced to come clean. In proof of his new statement he offered to show where the body of the dead chaukidar dacoit was. So he was sent in custody, with a Magistrate, to the village. He took the party to the patch of thick jungle about a mile from the village. A search was made and the sack containing the body was found buried in the jungle in about a foot of earth, the place of burial having been covered over with leaves and twigs. The body, or headless' trunk, was fully clothed, and had a dirty white blood-stained shirt on it, but on the shirt being removed, beneath it was found the blue blouse of a village policeman. Thus it was clear that the dead man was indeed none other than the missing chaukidar.

So in both cases, both the head of headless body and the body of the decapitated head were recovered. Unfortunately we could not restore the heads to the bodies, but at least in the case of the chaukidar, we could see that both body and head were cremated together. In this way the gods would be appeased and perhaps the soul of the village policeman saved from torment. We could not do the same, unfortunately, for the medical student for his body had to be burnt long before the head was recovered.

MOB-HYSTERIA

Almost the most embarrassing and terrifying experience which may face an officer connected with the administration of law and order is mob-hysteria. It is impossible to set out all the various situations which lead to hysteria in a mob, and once a mob is seized with hysteria, it is impossible to predict what form it will take, and by what actions it will express itself. The situation which leads to mob-hysteria may be the result of sudden happenings, or sudden ebullitions of feeling, or it may be the final result of an agitation which has been working up for some time.

The phenomenon of mob-hysteria can be found in any situation where feelings are suddenly worked up or aroused. While it is often seen in less advanced countries, it is experienced even in England, when something unexpected occurs among a large concourse of people, such as those gathered to watch athletic events. It may occur at a cinema hall if fire breaks out or amongst comparatively small crowds, gathered in connection with political meetings and processions.

On such occasions the mob has often collected without any set object or programme, frequently with no intention of committing any breach of the peace or causing any disorder. Some incident or speech, or the uttering of some slogan may suddenly enrage the mob, and in their insensate fury they may proceed to commit deeds that could not possibly have been foreseen or prevented. The individuals composing such mobs lose all sense of proportion, all reason and self-control. They act regardless of all consequences, and are utterly impervious to argument or persuasion. Often force is of no avail to stop their actions unless and until it results in physically incapacitating them. On more than one occasion I have

Rex Marsh-Smith, c.1912.

Kate Winifred Ellen Marsh-Smith,
always known as Winnie,
photographed at Lucknow.

The happiest day, February 9th, 1919.

The family home. A view from the garden.

The author, on the left, David Marsh-Smith, c.1924.

Police headquarters at Gwalior. Winnie and Rex Marsh-Smith garlanded for the camera.

The assembled Lucknow police officers, over fifty strong men.
Winnie with Patch the dog, Rex Marsh-Smith holds his dog Benjy by the collar.

Happy landing! The famous aviators Scott and Black arrive at Allahabad.

A confident party sets off to visit the Manipur Mela.
Winnie Marsh-Smith is seated on the central elephant.

On the way up in the
traditional way.
Motor cars also visible.

Rex Marsh-Smith in front of
the horseman directing the
proceedings at Ram Lila.

On parade. Rex Marsh-Smith inspects the militia.

At attention, Manipur camp, Gwalior State.

been requested by individuals in a mob struck by hysteria to shoot them. On occasions I have been invited to do so in almost polite language. The speakers have bared their chests and shouted, "Sir, please shoot us", and by their demeanour it was clear that they meant it.

Often mob-hysteria is induced by a feeling of frustration at not being able to achieve what the individuals of the mob thought they were going to achieve or what their leaders had promised them that they would achieve. They have been cheated of their goal, cheated of their reward, and their fury and indignation know no bounds.

On other occasions, when fear has caused the hysteria, in their mad desire to escape some danger, often imaginary, they ignore other and real dangers. They pay no heed to advice, instructions or warnings. To stop them you must take some physical action and, on some occasions, to save the lives of many, the lives of one or two persons have to be taken deliberately.

Another remarkable feature of mob-hysteria is that often, for some unaccountable reason, the hysteria ceases to operate. The mob halts its headlong fury, reason returns to the minds of individuals, they become normal, and will even join in the effort to control those still under the influence of hysteria. But more often the consequences of mob-hysteria are only prevented by physical force and by action of a drastic nature. It is only the really strong officer who can bring himself to take such action in time. Many a time the situation has been allowed to get out of control, and chaos resulted, because the man on the spot lost his nerve – was afraid to take the firm action which alone would have saved the situation. Very often he is afraid of the consequences to himself of taking such action, not so much the immediate consequences on the spot, as of what may happen to him and his career afterwards. He fears what his superiors may say and what the public may think. Much harm has been done by Commissions of Inquiry which have condemned the man on the spot and found him guilty of ruthless-ness, without a proper appreciation of the situation. They have not put themselves in the place of the officer faced with the problem of stopping a hysteria-driven mob. Officers have been induced by the findings of such commissions to have one eye on the mob and its doings and the other on the possible criticisms of higher authority. Only the really strong officer is able to take action guided by the requirements of the situation, regardless of possible censure by the public or his bosses.

In India, mob-hysteria is met with more frequently among the large crowds which collect at the time of religious processions and festivals, particularly when these crowds collect to bathe in a sacred river or pool. The psychological effect of such occasions is to imbue the minds of the mob with religious fervour and to dim their power of cool reasoning. Any sudden event has a speedy effect on their minds. I have known a catastrophic stampede being caused by the ground under the mob becoming soft like quicksand. People found themselves starting to sink in the mud. The stampede that ensued made the situation worse and lives were lost unnecessarily only because the mob was seized with hysteria.

Hardwar is one of the holiest spots in India. Here the river Ganges emerges from the low foothills of the Himalaya Range known as the Siwaliks. There is a holy pool at the river's edge known as the Har-ki-pairi. It is the place which draws the greatest number of Pilgrims in India. It contains innumerable temples, not only in the town and on the banks of the river, but also on many salient points on the surrounding hills, and even on the Islands mid-stream in the Ganges.

The permanent population of the town was about 45,000, but in the days appointed by the pandits as holy days for bathing, many thousands of pilgrims flocked to the town by rail and road. Every twelfth year is a Kumbh, when a large mela or bathing fair is held, and the number of pilgrims exceeds a million. All these persons went to Hardwar with the desire of bathing in the Har-ki-pairi pool. Not only an auspicious day, but an auspicious hour, nay, an auspicious minute is fixed at which the devout should immerse themselves in the holy water. This immersion has to take place in an area smaller than a football pitch.

The pool can, of course, only be approached from the land side, and there were only three very narrow roads which lead down to the pool, then reached by a flight of about sixty steps of stone about fifty feet wide.

One of the roads leading to these steps was on a gradient, and a particularly steep one at that. It was actually the main road through Hardwar from the plains through the Pass to the Dun, which is the country between the Siwaliks and the Himalaya. It is now a road about forty feet wide, metalled or cemented right through the town. Previously it was an ordinary somewhat ill-kept unmetalled road about twenty-five feet wide.

The Kumbh is the bathing festival celebrated every twelve years. It would take a volume in itself to describe the event and its setting, the huge crowds which started to collect for weeks before the sacred day, the camps set up on camping grounds fixed and regulated by Government and fitted with a proper water supply and even electric lighting, the gorgeous processions of sadhus (hermits) emanating from the various temple institutions in which the various sects of sadhus walk in akharas from their temple headquarters to the pool. The times for each of these processions to pass through the streets were worked out according to age-old custom and regulated by officials. Should these processions of the rival akharas meet, a clash would surely take place, and a bloody riot ensue, as indeed frequently happened in the olden days. The story would have to include a description of the elaborate arrangements which later had to be made by Government for the accommodation and feeding of these huge masses of people and providing sanitary arrangements for protection against disease and epidemics. A description of all these arrangements and of the mela itself, highly interesting and instructive though it would be, is not the purpose of this story.

This story is connected with the handling of part of the huge concourse, during a very short time. A small section of the crowd which had gathered on the sloping main street became seized with mob-hysteria.

The incident concerns a Kumbh mela which took place before the days of electricity, wireless communications and loud speakers, when telephones were, in India, in their infancy. The system of regulating the crowds depended on very primitive equipment. The problem was how to admit down to the pool the million or more people who wanted to bathe in it. Only about one thousand could be admitted to it at one time. There was always a danger of persons being carried away by the current. In those days, religious feeling demanded the minimum of interference with the flow of the water from the holy river. Any system of an effective barrier cutting off the pool from the main river would have been anathema. There was an equally serious danger to the crowds before ever they got to the pool, namely the danger of being crushed and trampled on in the narrow streets and on the flight of stone steps that led down to the pool. This danger was much enhanced by the steep gradient on the road from the Dun.

It was necessary to erect barriers along the roads and thus divide the oncoming crowds into pens as it were. The crowd from each of the three approach roads was then released towards the steps by turns. The barriers were made up of long wooden poles which had to be operated by pulleys worked by hand. They were pulled up from time to time on a given signal from a sort of control tower set up on the roofs of the houses overlooking the streets. These signals depended on good visibility, and although a system of lamp signalling had been tried, it proved difficult to operate.

It had been expected that the bathers would not come to the pool in great numbers before daylight, and arrangements were made for the police to come on duty about two o'clock in the morning. They would thus be, it was thought, early enough to control the early bathers. Unfortunately Dame Rumour took a hand. For some reason it got bruited abroad that the pandits had declared it would be a great act of piety to bathe twice, once before the Sadhus of the akharas had bathed, and once afterwards. Many decided to acquire merit by performing this double rite. In order to get a chance of so doing, they started making for the pool before midnight.

The police were hastily collected for duty two hours earlier than had been arranged. When the barriers and the control towers were manned it was found impossible to use the signals owing to poor visibility. The barriers had to be worked largely by guesswork and without signals, and there was naturally great difficulty in doing this.

The barriers could not be worked regularly. On the sloping road a great crowd had collected and got duly divided into pens, but in far greater numbers than was desirable from the point of view of safety. Eventually when the lowest barrier was lifted, the crowd rushed through. It was like lifting a flood-gate. All went well at first, then some old woman fell down and somebody fell over her. Soon there was a great crush. The crowds in the back pens got out of hand and opened the barriers themselves. The pressure from the back grew, and more and more people got knocked over. The pile of struggling humanity got breast-high.

No amount of reasoning or persuasion could induce the people at the back to stop. All were determined to press on to the pool and not to miss the opportunity of bathing at the auspicious time. Their fervour was uncontrollable. At length, seeing no other way out of the impasse, I literally forced my way to the top of the hill, knocking many people over on the way. I reached the top barrier and had it closed. I managed to secure some extra policemen from a nearby outpost to help those already there. I then returned to the lowest barrier where I found a writhing mass of persons.

This front barrier was manned by a force of police who were all Hindus with the exception of two European inspectors. They were assisted by a number of Boy Scouts and Volunteers, who were also all Hindus. These Hindus, volunteers and police alike, refused to assist in extricating the living from the dead. They were afraid of being contaminated and outcasted for touching a dead body. It was left to the two Europeans to separate the living from the dead, and thus save many of the former from being suffocated and swelling the numbers of the latter.

Eventually the task was completed. The number of casualties was great. Twenty-three persons were already dead and over one hundred more were in a precarious state. After the work of separation was over the Hindus, police and volunteers then came forward to do their duty and render first aid to the living. They then worked like heroes in arranging the conveyance of the wounded to the hospital. No motor ambulances in those days! The wounded all had to be conveyed on stretchers carried by these men on foot.

Only then was order restored, and the normal control of the crowds resumed. I was a very junior officer, though saddled with a great responsibility. Thinking of what my superiors might say, and what the public would think, I was brooding over the matter and bemoaning my position, bewailing the fact that twenty-three persons had lost their lives before daybreak. What would be the total before the end of the day? Then an old Sadhu, who was there unhurt, came to me and said:

> "Sahib, what are you worrying about? By stopping the oncoming crowd you saved many lives, though you knocked some persons over in the process. Moreover what better fate could a good Hindu ask for than to die at the foot of the Har-ki-pairi?"

Fortunately no more serious casualties occurred that day, though more than a million persons passed through the pool, and the police were continuously on duty for twenty-four hours.

At the next Kumbh, twelve years later, there was a similar tragedy as a result of mob-hysteria. This occurred on one of the mid-stream islands. This island was of a considerable area, but ordinarily not inhabited, as it was liable to inundation when the Ganges got swollen in the rains. On the occasion of these large melas it afforded a spacious, though far from comfortable, camping-ground for pilgrims. It was reached across a branch of the river by a temporary pontoon bridge about twelve feet wide.

The cause of the panic on this occasion was a sudden outbreak of fire in the middle of the night in the jungle and undergrowth on the island. This fire spread to part of the camping-ground and caused a simultaneous stampede of about fifty thousand people on the island who all made a mad rush to the pontoon bridge. Actually the fire only affected a small part of the island, but the noise of the fire and the size of the flames in the jungle generated uncontrollable panic among the pilgrims. The stampede rapidly got beyond the control of the police on the island. In a very short time the bridge got over-crowded and collapsed under the weight of the people scurrying across it. The mob, thinking themselves threatened by the fire, threw themselves in numbers into the river. Complete hysteria prevailed, and the situation was only restored with great difficulty by rushing reinforcements of police over to the island in boats. The number of persons drowned in the river could never be accurately ascertained but some hundreds perished.

On very many occasions in India, mobs actuated by religious animosity or anti-government feeling, have acted in a most insensate manner and committed all sorts of horrible deeds. On these occasions it was largely the result of their feelings being lashed into fury, a state of affairs somewhat different from mob-hysteria. The mob was not actuated by any panic or fear of injury to themselves. They, it is true, may have originally collected with no intent to commit violence and then some speech or incident caused their fury to burst into flame.

Such was the case when, in Cawnpore, riots originating as anti-British became communal and spread all over the city. In a few days the resulting casualties numbered over one thousand, an unheard of number up to that time, but since dwarfed by the tragic communal slaughter which followed Partition. During this unfortunate period of 1942 mobs collected in several districts and attacked police stations and treasuries, committing murders, arson, and loot. All these mobs were actuated by hostile feelings which had been worked up, and they became uncontrollable. At many places resolute action might have saved the situation, and often did, but the forces of law and order present were often quite insufficient. Eventually only the arrival of sufficient forces of police and military could restore order.

Still more terrible results of mob action were seen in the days following the partition of India, starting in the Punjab and spreading to many parts of India. These days saw casualties in numbers which far exceeded those of the Cawnpore riots mentioned above. They indeed exceeded the total casualties, civil and military, suffered by Britain in the five years of the second World War, and that in the space of a few weeks. Crowds of the major community collected and wrought havoc with the lives and property of the members of the minor community. The slaughter and rapine only ceased when the supply of victims dried up owing to the headlong flight of the minor community. The crowds collected were absolutely bereft of reason and control. Literally hundreds of thousands lost their lives or were injured, and millions were forced to flee their homes and leave their all. The total extent of these dire calamities will never be known, and time alone can wipe out the memory of that ghastly period of carnage, when a form of mob-hysteria enveloped huge areas of the sub-continent.

However these situations did not always have the dire results of the Cawnpore riots of 1931, still less of the partition riots of 1947. I have a pleasant recollection, tinged with the utmost thankfulness to the Almighty, of such a situation which unaccountably came to an end without a single casualty.

This also concerned the city of Cawnpore. It was on the occasion of the arrest of a great and much-revered figure in Indian politics of the day. Hearing of that event, huge crowds turned out in the streets as a mark of protest. The main thoroughfares got blocked with crowds of pedestrians, all of whom came out simultaneously and spontaneously to show their respect for their leader, and their disgust at his arrest. They were not making for any particular meeting place. In fact, in those days, there was no acknowledged meeting place capable of accommodating anything like the large concourse of people out in the streets. More than one hundred thousand people must have come out. There were no speakers or set speeches as there was no meeting as such. Here and there orators got up on some improvised platforms and harangued the crowds moving up and down the streets. But the very absence of a programme and of a fixed aim made the situation all the more fraught with dangerous possibilities. At any moment some speech of one of these street orators, some deed or action on the part of some unthinking or harassed police official, might have acted as a spark to set off their fury and to start mob-hysteria among them. Goodness knows what would have been the result if that spark had been set off and they had been overcome with mob-hysteria.

I had been called in from tour and had to pass through the city with my wife in the car with me. In fact when we got to the centre of the city I had to drop off and leave her to drive home – a step which I took with some qualms, but 1 knew she should would have the nerve to do it all right, and she did. The crowds were by that time really excited, shouting slogans, and raising their arms, but they were not armed with any weapons of violence. This fact, in itself, made the situation very difficult to deal with. With crowds everywhere and all unarmed, if force was to be used, where was a start to be made? And how was it to be called off?

We were almost at our wits end to hit upon some means of getting the people to leave the streets and go home. Suddenly I conceived the idea of letting it be known that an order had been passed that everybody found in the streets after dark (then about 7 p.m.) would be arrested. In later years much use came to be made of similar orders which quickly came to be known as 'curfew orders', and which actually had the sanction of the Criminal Procedure Code.

On this occasion, somewhat to our surprise and much to our relief, the expedient worked like magic. The word went round the crowds in the streets and gradually the idea of possible arrest permeated the almost hysterical crowds. They quietened down, stopped shouting and crying out slogans, and gradually left the streets and went off home. In an hour the streets were cleared, and the city resumed its normal night life.

Whew!! We wiped our brows, and it was with a sigh of thanksgiving and utter relief that I turned to the District Magistrate and said:

"Let's first thank God for the miracle and then go home and have a drink".

I think we had deserved several, and we had 'em.

WE LAUGH LAST

Proceed at once and take command of combined operations against Randhir Singh.

This was the telegraphic message I received from His Highness the Maharajah, when I was inspecting a district some three hundred miles away from the area which I knew Randhir Singh was exploiting.

Randhir Singh was an outlaw whose father had been murdered by men of the opposing faction in the village. The persons accused of the murder, which had been done in broad daylight, had been duly arrested by the local police and sent up for trial, but all had been acquitted by the Session Judge. Randhir Singh's party alleged that large sums of money had changed hands, and hence this miscarriage of justice. Randhir Singh decided that there was no hope of justice from what he called a corrupt police and judiciary, and that there was nothing for it but to take the law into his own hands. So one day he took out his gun and shot the two chief accused who had been acquitted. He found them ploughing their fields, and so they proved a sitting target. He then disappeared from his village and went underground.

These murders and counter-murders had occurred some years before the day on which I received the telegraphic message. In the meanwhile Randhir Singh had formed a gang of dacoits who had been looting the countryside for about three years. He lived in a village which was in a jungle tract for which a scheme of colonisation had been formulated, as part of the far-sighted policy of His Highness's gifted father, and which some residents of the Punjab had been invited to develop. Attracted by the easy terms on which the land was offered, they had come along. The scheme included an irrigation project which for some reason or other had not come to fruition. Consequently the area remained undeveloped and there were but few villages in the area. No metalled roads had been driven through it, and it remained very inaccessible. The district authorities seldom visited it and the Police patrolling was deficient and inefficient.

Consequently it was not long before Randhir Singh had established a reign of terror in the locality. Randhir Singh first established his reputation by committing dacoities at night on the houses of the few well-to-do families of the area. Later he set up a sort of assassination agency, which was ready to bump off people who were unacceptable to those who were willing to pay for them to be put out of the way. Another profitable method of crime was to kidnap some wealthy person, often the young son of the village banker, and then negotiate with his relatives for a ransom. In course of time Randhir Singh had amassed a considerable sum of money, and had acquired a veritable arsenal of guns and rifles of various descriptions. Frequently he committed dacoities with the sole object of obtaining such weapons and ammunition.

When I first arrived to take over the police administration of the area he had already committed more than one hundred murders, dacoities, robberies, kidnappings and cattle liftings. His reputation for daring was legendary and his game had been made easier by purchasing the benevolent neutrality of the local police. This, I found later, he had been able to do in full measure.

I had laid on all the various methods of preventing these crimes such as patrolling by special armed police, but these had only served to put a stop to the occurrences for temporary periods. The perpetrators had not been arrested and crime broke out afresh as soon as the crafty local sub-inspector could work out a scheme to keep the gang away from the areas he was patrolling on orders. So nothing was being achieved by these measures and the Headquarters staff, stationed nearly three hundred miles away, had to set to and devise some method which could be concealed from the local police. For this purpose it was necessary to enlist special agents who were sent out in disguise to join the gang and obtain inside information about its movements and plans and the habits of the leaders. This last was important, for almost invariably it is weakness for "wine women and song" which provides the means by which such gangs are lured to their downfall.

The acquisition of secret intelligence about criminal gangs in this way is a dangerous job, and the persons employed, if they are to be successful, must literally take their life in their hands. The job calls for the use of the utmost resourcefulness, courage and tact, to say nothing of a high degree of histrionic ability. Initial failure makes a subsequent attempt even more difficult, and in this case we met with disaster at the early stages of our campaign.

About ten days after we had sent out our agents a report was received from one of the police stations in the area to the effect that an unidentified corpse had been found in the jungle. Death had been caused by gun-shot and the body had been badly mutilated. Fearing the worst, I sent out a police officer from Headquarters who soon came back with the news that the murdered man was one of our agents. The officer who came to report said,

> "Sahib, that darogha (sub-inspector) is a namak haram (untrue to his salt). Unfortunately, Sant Ram, the agent had disclosed his identity and mission to him, and he must have got into touch with Randhir Singh and put him wise as to who this man was. Randhir Singh must have murdered him out of hand. I am very sorry about this for Sant Ram was one of my best men and he leaves a wife and two children who will now have to be provided for".

> "I am, sorry for the family", I said, "but this has put a spoke in all our plans and we shall have to withdraw all our agents lest they suffer a like fate. But we must move that rascally darogha, Sunder Lal, to a less healthy and less lucrative clime".

And this, indeed, we had perforce to do, and bide our time. Meanwhile Randhir Singh also had to suspend operations for fear that there were other agents who might bring about his capture. He almost certainly had been warned by the local police that he must keep quiet for a while. Then a transfer of the sub-inspector must have made him let up, at least until he had ascertained the calibre of his successor, and renewed his accommodation with the local police. Thus it came about that, in spite of the non-arrest of Randhir Singh, these crimes ceased. As a matter of fact Randhir Singh thought it would be a good idea to pay a visit to his homeland in the Punjab.

As for me, I turned my attention to the many other pressing tasks that awaited me, and in due course proceeded on tour to the distant part of my jurisdiction, where I received the telegram.

Randhir Singh, after a few months' holiday, had returned to his village. He had wrongly assumed that he could square the new darogha who, however, was fly enough to have given him that impression. Randhir Singh came along to his own house thinking it was perfectly safe to do so.

However the local police chief "wasn't having any". As soon as he got to know of the return of Randhir Singh, he proceeded to the village with a posse of police with the idea of pulling in Randhir Singh and his chief lieutenants. Unfortunately he was not fully aware of the resources of the brigand leader. A direct attack on his house, a sort of small fort, known as a garhi, was at once met with an outburst of firing.

The sub-inspector now took stock of the situation and realised that he had bitten off more than he could chew. He could get no help from the villagers who were too much afraid of Randhir Singh. So he had to send to district headquarters for assistance. The District Officer was well aware of the strength of the gang, and, incidentally, of the strategic position of Randhir Singh's garhi on rising ground in the village. He had, at his headquarters, a regiment of Cavalry and he had authority to demand assistance from the Commanding Officer. That Officer, perhaps exaggerating the situation, and realising that the job was not one for a cavalry unit, had sent a message to Army Headquarters asking for some infantry. Nevertheless he immediately dispatched a squadron of his unit to the village. From Headquarters was dispatched a company of infantry as well as some extra police from the Headquarters Reserve. Meanwhile the Ruler, who always kept in personal touch with everything that was going on and was ever solicitous for the welfare of his subjects, decided that it was desirable to have his highest police officer in charge of the combined operation. Thus it came about that the telegram was sent to me, four hundred miles away from headquarters, and three hundred miles from the village.

Fortunately I had a police lorry with me and I travelled through the night, arriving at the road-head early in the morning. From there it was necessary to proceed on foot for the remaining twelve miles through the jungle. Owing to the difficulty of the terrain, it was well into the night by the time I arrived at the outskirts of the village.

On my arrival, my second-in-command, who had come from Headquarters, reported to me that the village was absolutely surrounded on all sides by military and police, and that Randhir Singh and his men were still in his house fortress. There had been desultory firing for three days and two policemen had become casualties (one of them subsequently dying of wounds he had received). Nobody, however, would take the responsibility of a direct assault, either by police or military, until I came.

As it was now past midnight, I contented myself with going round the village and satisfying myself that the cordon was complete. I decided to wait till daybreak before carrying out a personal reconnaissance of the position. There was no hurry and no point in taking hasty steps, for was not the gang safely bottled up? Satisfied with the situation, I returned to that part of the line covered by police, and commandeered a charpoy (small string bed) on which to snatch a few hours' sleep.

Meantime I reflected on the situation. Here was a force consisting of one squadron of cavalry, a company of infantry, and the equivalent of a company of police. Surely sufficient at least to provide an impregnable line through which the small gang of perhaps six or seven dacoits could not possibly try to escape, however desperate they might be. True there had been some lack of initiative shown by the officers in the past twenty-four hours. However, I was now quite sure that a few hours' daylight would see the operation brought to a successful close. It was the height of the cold weather and not having been able to bring my bedding with me, I felt the cold intensely, even with my greatcoat on, and I naturally would not have got much sleep. In fact I had hardly settled down, when a burst of firing was heard *outside* the perimeter of the village. What this could mean I could not conceive. Were not the dacoits *inside* the village? I dispatched a police party to investigate the cause of the firing. On their return this party reported that the firing was due to a false alarm. The tehsildar had gone off to arrange for supplies for the troops, and had been accompanied by an armed escort. When, on the way back, they had seen, or thought they had seen, some persons moving in the jungle and they had let off their guns, really in panic. This was an indication of the nervous state of the surrounding force. I learnt that an altogether exaggerated idea of the strength of the gang had got among the troops. Perhaps they were not to be blamed for this, considering the strength of the force sent out to deal with them. Perhaps this also explained the failure to take the initiative, and the decision to await my arrival, and I now began to understand the reason for the delay. Actually for the rest of the night there were no more alarms and rumours, and the day broke with the position unchanged.

At daybreak I summoned the officers of the units for a conference, and to get first-hand reports of what had transpired. It appeared that there had been a considerable amount of firing on both sides during the first day of the siege but this had greatly decreased in tHe last twenty-four hours. These officers confirmed that the reason for no direct assault having been made was that orders had been received that this was not to be done till I arrived. The idea was, no doubt, that it was probable that unnecessary loss of life would be avoided in this way.

The day was opened by a renewal of single shots from the house but it was impossible to gauge on what target they were directed. I then decided to move up near to the house and try to see the position for myself. If the story of the amount of firing done by the dacoits was correct, they would not have much ammunition left. There was, therefore, in spite of what was being urged on me, little danger in making an approach. So I took an armed police constable with me and gradually advanced from point to point up the rising ground toward the gate. Some more shots were fired but not, I think, in our direction. We proceeded right up to the gate. Nothing

79

happened. The gate doorway was not locked or bolted, so we passed in. To my astonishment there seemed to be no human being about. There were the usual domestic animals in the yard. We proceeded to go into the main building which eventually also proved to be empty except in one of the rooms where, to my surprise, was a young woman – later ascertained to be the wife of Randhir Singh. Randhir Singh and his gang had just vanished, and the wife was not saying anything as to their whereabouts.

It was evident that they had cleared out, leaving the woman behind with instruction to fire off occasionally in the air the two muzzle-loading weapons which were left behind. They had taken all their other guns with them. She had just about finished her powder and shot when we came into the room.

After this surprising denouement I went back to the officers and told them the position. They were naturally astounded to hear that Randhir Singh was not there and much ashamed that he had somehow succeeded in hoodwinking them. However, it seemed that there was nothing to be done but to remove the small army back to Headquarters. But before arrangements could be made to do this a further incident occurred. A local villager came along with a letter addressed to me. It was written in Hindi, purported to come from Randhir Singh and had been written in a village about ten miles off. It read:

> You think yourself a great officer, and you thought you had got me in a trap. But I am much too clever for the likes of you and your troops are all cowards. Fancy you thinking you could get me like that; well, you haven't a hope. I am a much bigger man than you and am not afraid of you or of any of your forces. What's more I've sworn an oath that 1 will first go to district headquarters and cut off the head of the District Officer. I will then come to your bungalow in the Capital, and will cut off your head also. And this I will do in a very short time. Take whatever steps you like, you won't be able to stop me.

This letter was, of course, sheer bravado, but it indicated the frame of mind into which the brigand chief had got himself. The sheer audacity of his escape and the episode of the threatening

A 'mugger' shooting. Pat Biggie, Wyn Lewys-Lloyd and Rex Marsh-Smith
set off to shoot crocodiles under the Christmas sun.

A crocodile is arrested! Ram Lall, bearer to Rex Marsh-Smith is on the left
of the group.

Crossing the Chambal River in the Christmas sun.

Hampers and bottles. Picnic conversation.

Winnie, Rex Marsh-Smith, Wyn Lewys-Lloyd and Pop Fuller
ride the elephant under a Christmas sun.

Rex Marsh-Smith presides at table at the Manipur camp.

Gwalior police recruits at Chrismas camp.

Frank Mudie, Rex and Winnie Marsh-Smith, Connie Everett,
Christmas time.

A very sombre occasion. The official farewell by Gwalior police officers, Gwalior, 18th December 1948.

Sitting: C. S. Kadam, S. V. Chauhan, B. B. Patil, D. P. Thorat, Bhairon Singh, D. N. Deo, G. B. Jachak, R. N. Marsh-Smith I.P., C.S.I.C.I.E., Pt. Jagannath, Pd. Gopal Sahai, Khizar Mohd., K. S. Sahestrabudhdhe, Nagu, G. W. Deshmukh, Ram Swarup Tiwari.

Standing, 1st row: S. K. Sahastrabudhdhe, R. R. Bhousle, Sambhar Singh, P. Pund, Pokhan Singh, J. N. Dar, V. D. Dubey, Daljit Singh, Virendra Singh, K. V. Bhajekar, N. A. Nagarkar, V. K. Gupta, S. H. Chowdhary, N. R. Bombley, Mahesh Pd., Shaefat Khan, D. K. Raje.

Standing, 2nd row: Chotey Lal, P. B. Shinde, R. R. Singh, Kanchan Singh, Sardar Singh, Ganesh Singh, Kashi Prasad, K. C. Dixit, R. C. Chaturvedi, C. R. Mukerjee, L. S. Astade, Jai Narain, Yakoob Khan, D. P. Tyagi, G. P. Chaturvedi, K. B. Ingle.

The Maharajah of Gwalior.
A rare signed photograph given to Rex Marsh-Smith, 1939.

The end of an era.
A happy Rex Marsh-Smith
in the late forties.

Medal Ceremony, Rex Marsh-Smith on the right, surveys the assembly.

Top row from left: Companion Indian Empire Medal,
Companion Star of India Kaiser-i-hind Medal,
and Medal belonging to Kate Winifred Ellen.

Central row: Dress Medals.

Bottom row, from left:
King's Police Medal with bar; Indian Police Medal, c1933,
both for gallantry; 3rd and 4th, Service Medals.

letter had raised his reputation to a dazzling height, and also enhanced the awe with which he was looked upon, not only by the people of the countryside, but also by the local petty officials. This would make the task of rounding him up all the more difficult.

The restoration of the prestige of the forces of law and order was now imperative. I came to the conclusion that Randhir Singh had got swollen headed, as witnessed by his bravado in sending that impudent letter, and possibly he would become careless. On this assumption we made our further dispositions. We had, in the meanwhile, through the courage of some of our detectives, got to know a good deal more about his contacts and habits. In particular we learnt that he had a passion for a certain Beria prostitute in the village from which he had sent his letter of defiance. We accordingly established, very secretly, contact with this lady. Quite a large sum of money was spent, and in the end she promised to summon Randhir Singh and his merry men to a big party. She invited him to come along and celebrate his victory over the 'foreign' police General. Acting closely in conjunction with the new darogha, she arranged a really good party, and the darogha was given instructions to step in and collar the gang when they were really drunk.

All went well this time and according to plan. Randhir Singh fell for the bait. He went along with all the important lads of his gang and did they have a beano! The wine flowed, the food was good and the music seductive. The ladies were most gracious. The drinking and carousing went on well into the night. The brigand chief and his men succumbed completely, and all, one after another, sank to the floor, blind to the world; in fact down and out.

Our darogha was taking no chances. First he had managed to get a drug put in the drink late in the evening, and that was why the drinkers went out so completely. Then, when they were all in this condition, he and his men went in and shot the lot.

Thus within fifteen days of his bombastic threat, Randhir met his fate. Nemesis overtook him and instead of my head and that of the District Officer being cut off and carried away by him, the bodies of Randhir Singh and his six lieutenants were brought to me in triumph by the sub-inspector.

The lady of easy virtue had done her job well and fully earned her wages. Admittedly the final action of the local police was perhaps indefensible, but one can hardly blame them for taking no risks. At least I was not going to question their action. The gang, and its chief, who had been the terror of the countryside and had committed countless crimes of violence, rape, and pillage were brought to book. Above all, the prestige of the forces of law and order had been restored. I was content to leave it at that.

It remains to relate how Randhir Singh had been spirited away out of the village surrounded by units of the army and police, sufficient to cover every yard of the perimeter. The clue to this mystery was to be found in the personnel of some of the surrounding troops. In the squadron of cavalry which first reached the village, there was a section of Punjabis who hailed from the same village in the Punjab which was Randhir Singh's original home. When he found himself invested, he saw that his only chance lay in getting in touch with these men and inducing them to help him. So it happened that in the dead of the night before I reached the village, this section of Punjab soldiers had allowed Randhir Singh and his men to pass through their section of the line and get away.

So Randhir Singh had the laugh of us, cavalry, infantry and police – all of whom failed to prevent his escape. However, as the adage says, "He laughs best who laughs last".

We had the last laugh.

AN INSIDE JOB

It was in the early years between the two World Wars and I was in charge of an out-of-the-way district about sixty miles from an important military station. It was the cold weather and I was on tour in the interior of the district, incidentally enjoying myself immensely with the excellent shooting in the locality: duck, snipe and partridge galore! It was with the utmost regret that I had to leave the area hastily to look into an important crime about which urgent information was brought to me by special messenger.

This man brought a letter from the Officer Commanding the British Infantry Regiment stationed in the cantonments of the neighbouring district. He and his battalion were on exercise at a camp in my district, unfortunately in a different location. The letter was a formal one and ran somewhat as follows:

> *I regret to have to report that a serious crime has taken place In the camp where this unit is on exercise. Last night the strong-box containing Government and regimental funds was removed from the tent of the Headquarters Guard. The box contained about Rs 90,000* (the equivalent of £6,000 in those days), *including the pay of the men in camp which had only been brought in from the District Treasury that afternoon.*
>
> *I request that an investigation be instituted immediately and I consider that the matter is one which demands your personal attention.*

The letter was signed by the Adjutant of the Battalion on behalf of the Commanding Officer. The news entailed the immediate striking of my camp and my return to Headquarters, leaving, with great reluctance, some of the best shooting I have had the good fortune to enjoy. From Headquarters I had to proceed another thirty miles, but the camp was on a main provincial road so, unusually in those days, I was able to take my car. Nevertheless forty-eight hours had passed since the discovery of the theft before I could reach the scene.

The camp, in the shape of a rectangle, was situated about one hundred yards off the main road. There were six companies of the battalion in camp and each had its own guard in a tent, while there was a Headquarters guard in a tent next to the guard-tent of A. Coy. There were thus seven sentries round the perimeter of the camp. The strong-box, a fairly heavy wooden box, had been placed in the Headquarters guard tent.

On the Friday afternoon an escort, consisting of an officer and N.C.O. and four soldiers, had brought the pay of the men in camp from the district Headquarters (about thirty miles away) in a military lorry, and had duly deposited approximately Rs 80,000 in the strong-box. This already contained Rs 10,000 of battalion money. Most of the money was in currency notes of various denominations. On Saturday morning the corporal of the Headquarters guard had found the strong-box missing. It had just vanished during the night. He duly reported the loss to the Adjutant who at once told the Commanding Officer.

The whole staff were dumbfounded by the loss and particularly by the mysterious manner in which it had taken place. All sorts of rumours were afloat, but the general idea in the battalion was that some very clever native thieves had succeeded in entering the tent and carrying off the box. Various men came forward with stories of having heard rustling sounds, and even of seeing natives with oiled bodies crawling through the grass. The C.O. had organised a search of the whole camp and of the vicinity of the perimeter. Eventually, by the time I had arrived, the strong-box had been found about one hundred yards off the road in the jungle on the opposite side. It had been broken open and all the cash and notes had been removed, but cheque books and account books had been left.

This was the position when I arrived at the camp and met the C.O. He told me all the salient features of the case and proceeded to dilate on the certainty of the theft having been the work of his canteen contractor's agent and his men. He was, of course, much impressed by the many stories given him about natives having been seen moving about the perimeter at night.

It so happened that in those days there was a notorious gang of dacoits operating over a wide area in those parts. They had committed innumerable robberies and murders and were known to belong mostly to a gang of nomadic criminals. There was a special police organisation under the leadership of a famous police officer* appointed to hunt down this gang. The C.O. was bitten with the idea that his canteen contractor's agent had got in touch with this gang and called them in to commit this daring crime.

"Mark my words", he said to me, "You will find that fellow is behind this affair. I have always distrusted him and you have only to check up on him and you will come on to something".

My mind was running in a completely different direction and I had been much influenced by a point which was self-evident from the circumstances of the case. The particular night on which the crime was committed was the only night on which success was possible. Most of the money had only come in that afternoon and was to have been distributed to the men next day. In answer to the C.O. I said:

> "Maybe it's as you think, colonel, and I'll not leave any avenue unexplored, but somehow I don't think you are right, We'll have to look nearer home".
>
> "What!" he said, almost exploding "Do you suspect any of my men? The idea' s preposterous.

Almost dramatically, apparent confirmation of his theory was forthcoming. One of my officers came along at that moment and reported that one of the stolen notes had been impounded at a shop in a nearby town.

"There you are", said the C.O. in triumph. "How could my men

* *This was Freddie Young, a colleague of my father. The dacoit was Sultana and the investigation was featured in the film "The Long Duel" staring Trevor Howard and Yul Brunner. DM-S*

have got to dispose of the stolen notes? Clearly outsiders have done this and are getting rid of the notes as soon as they can".

This certainly did seem confirmation of his theory and I accordingly had the contractor's agent and his men all thoroughly searched, and their movements checked up, but nothing was discovered. Nevertheless the C.O. strongly objected to inquiries being pursued on the basis of the complicity of anyone in the regiment. So we came to a temporary deadlock.

Meanwhile several other notes were recovered in the locality and a number of persons were arrested for being in possession of stolen property. By a strange coincidence, however, an event occurred which revolutionised the whole inquiry. A report was received from a railway station down the line that a one hundred rupee note bearing the same number as the series of notes shown as stolen from the strong-box of the regiment had been handed in at a certain hour. Calculation showed that, if this note had been stolen from the strong-box on the Friday night in question, it could not have reached the railway station concerned by the time the note was handed in!

This fact put a different complexion on the whole matter and gave rise to doubts as to the correctness of the numbers of the notes given as the numbers of the stolen notes. Accordingly I decided to make a check at the Treasury personally. Armed with the memo which had been given to the Officer in charge of the escort, I went to the Treasury Officer and said:

> "Are you sure that the memo which was prepared of the numbers of the notes given to the regiment was correct"?
>
> "Yes", he said. "I prepared it personally. Why? What makes you question it?"

I told him of the apparently contradictory position in respect of the note impounded at the far railway station. I suggested that we should go to the strong room of the Treasury and check up the memo there. So we went along and he examined the pigeon holes, each of which contained a block of notes to the value of Rs 10,000. As he was checking, he was reading aloud the numbers shown on the memo. Suddenly he came to a stop and said:

"Good heavens! One of the blocks of notes shown in the memo is still here!"

Sure enough it was. A further check revealed what had happened. In noting down the letters of the note numbers they had been shown as X B over Y instead of X B over Z. Actually many of the X B over Y series were still in the pigeon hole. Thus it came about that the notes which had been recovered or handed in were not, in fact, the stolen notes at all.

This meant not only that the various persons who had been taken into custody were innocent and must be released, but still more important, that ideas as to the responsibility for the theft had to be recast. In particular, although this discovery did not preclude the possibility of the correctness of the C.O.'s theory, it did mean that the stolen notes had yet to be recovered, and indicated that the thieves might not yet have been able to dispose of them. Thus we were brought back to the idea of an inside job. I was, now able to persuade the C.O. to allow me to make further inquiries in the unit.

I started with the rather perfunctory step of examining the strong-box for finger-prints and requested the C.O. to let me take the finger-prints of the men of the escort and of the Headquarters guard for comparison. Although I pointed out that it was largely a matter of elimination more than anything else, he strongly demurred to this, but eventually agreed.

When, however, it came to taking the prints of the officer in charge of the escort, that was more than he could stomach and he flatly refused to allow it. Nothing was to be gained by insistence and I then went on with the next step in the inquiry which I wanted to take. Though I feared he would not agree, I said:

"I want to take the statement of everyone in the camp as to their movements on the night of the theft".

To my surprise he replied, "Go ahead, but what you are going to get out of it I cannot think".

I hadn't a very clear idea myself, but luck was, to some extent with me.

I was allotted a separate tent in which to carry out this

interrogation and the Adjutant and the R.S.M. were told to help me. The procedure was to bring in each man, one at a time. The man made his statement and marched off, generally passing the next man at the door of the tent.

The interrogation was going along smoothly and without incident, but without anything useful being elicited. I was drumming with my fingers against the underneath of the table at which I sat. "Tap-tap-tap" went my fingers, out of nervousness or, perhaps, sheer boredom and disappointment at the apparent failure of the operation. I had finished questioning one of the men, and as he went out I heard him say to the next man coming in, "Look out, that detective bloke has got a dictaphone under the table!"

I immediately halted the interrogation and ascertained the names of these two men. They were Private Jones and Private Brown. I asked for their kits to be searched. In Brown's kit were found a suit of "civvies" and a revolver, neither of which articles was it lawful, in those days, for a private soldier to possess. Otherwise nothing incriminating or directly connecting them with the theft was found. Nor was anything further got out of the interrogation which, however, was laboriously completed.

Soon after, the battalion was to march back to its station. They were to march by the metalled road which passed through the town which was the headquarters of my district, and were to halt there for the night. We had searched all the kits of the battalion after the Jones-Brown incident and found nothing more, and, I now suggested to the C.O. that we should make another search in case the thieves had resumed possession of the notes. He readily agreed, convinced as he still was that his men were not responsible and the search would give another opportunity to clear them. The C.O. was pleased and so was I. He because he thought his men were now finally cleared, I because I was now sure that the money had not been moved with the battalion. Would attempts be made to move it hereafter?

Next morning the battalion resumed its march homewards. The affair of the disappearance of the strong-box was apparently to remain an unsolved mystery. In the regiment, and indeed throughout the British units of the garrison, there was much talk about the theft and many ideas were ventilated as to the fate of the money. Many were the stories and rumours circulated about it. The money got to be known in military circles as 'the treasure'. Much of this talk reached my ears and seemed to confirm my idea that the affair was an inside job.

Soon I got to hear of ventures to make search for the 'treasure' and these made me convinced that the money had not left the vicinity of the camp.

I accordingly left some keen young detective constables in the area near the camp with instructions to watch for any possible attempt to move the money. I had no idea of where, in this area, it might have been secreted, and so could not watch any particular locality. It had necessarily to be somewhere near the camp site and might be within a radius of a mile or two.

I further arranged with the chief of the police where the battalion was stationed that all stories appearing to have any bearing on the treasure and its whereabouts should be passed on to me.

The first thing that transpired concerned the proprietor of a sort of restaurant in the Cantonments which was open to the troops. This man had a motor car which he had recently purchased from an officer leaving India. This car was one of the few in the whole garrison and the only one which could be hired. A few other cars belonged to officers. The transaction over the car, and perhaps mismanagement of his business, had landed the proprietor in debt. He was very familiar with the soldiers of the Garrison and took good care to keep in with both the military and civil police. In fact he was rather a shady character.

One day, in casual conversation with a civil police European Sergeant, he mentioned an incident which appeared to have some bearing on the 'treasure'. A private soldier of the infantry regiment had approached him for the hire, or rather loan, of his car. So keen was this man on obtaining the use of a car that he actually offered to clear all the debts of the owner which amounted to about Rs 1,500 (fifty pounds) for the loan of the car for the whole day. Although the transaction was clearly a fishy one, the owner was quite prepared to agree, but the deal fell through over the question of a driver. The owner was only prepared to hire out the car provided he was to drive it. He was not prepared to let anyone else drive it. This would mean that the soldier would have to divulge the destination and purpose of the journey for which the car was required, and the soldier was not prepared to let him know this. Although he related the whole story to the police sergeant, he was not willing to give out the name of the soldier. In fact he pretended that he did not know his name. This incident, though of possible significance, did not give us much to go on. I thought at the time that the restaurant proprietor was telling the truth when he said that he did not know the reason for which the car was to be borrowed.

Soon after, however, a more revealing and direct incident occurred. One of the constables put on to watch near the camp came post-haste to me when I was again on tour in another part of the district. He said to me:

"Huzur (Your Honour), I was, according to your instructions, on duty at the little wayside railway station. I was watching the passengers coming and going by the early morning train. By that train a gora (pale face, which was the term sometimes applied to Britishers in India, particularly to soldiers) boarded the train for the cantonment station, and booked a cycle in the luggage van. He was wearing mufti dress like a sahib, but I am sure we was not an officer or an official. He did not have a sporting gun with him so he had not come for a shikar".

This was an interesting piece of information. That a soldier should have been alone in these parts at this time so early in the morning was, indeed, strange, and that he had arrived with a cycle was significant. The fact that he had no gun with him showed that he had not come for shooting and in any case it was most unlikely that he should come alone for that purpose. The fact that he took a ticket for the cantonment where the battalion which had lost the money was stationed indicated some possible connection with that affair. I accordingly decided that the matter was worth pursuing personally.

It was first necessary to establish the identity of the man who had travelled by train with a cycle. Out of the many possibilities I decided to plump for this man being a soldier. If the cycle was privately owned the matter would be difficult. If, however, it was a hired one, a check-up on the cycle dealers should reveal something. I accordingly deputed a special staff for the purpose. After a laborious search, the following item of information was secured:

On the day before the departure from the railway station near the camp of the men with the cycle, two cycles had been hired by two Europeans who came in civilian clothes and took over the cycles. They had been signed in the register with a signature that was almost illegible but which appeared to be "A.J. Smith". The dealer said he would be able to identify the men if they were produced before him in civilian clothes. The most interesting part of the information, however, was that only one cycle was brought back. "Mr Smith" had been back and admitted responsibility for the second one and had promised to pay compensation for it. Who was this Smith?

In the search for him a rule which was then in force in the military units helped us considerably. Only an N.C.O. employed on staff duties outside his unit was allowed to wear mufti when off duty. A check on the men so employed led us to the Brigade Office. We arranged with the Brigadier that the British staff (other than Officers) would be put up for identification by the cycle dealer. This was duly arranged and he unhesitatingly picked out two corporals named Pritchard and Robinson as the two men who had hired the cycles, and the former as the man who had signed the hire register. In spite of this identification, these two men denied any knowledge of the cycles. So some witnesses from the wayside railway station were called to see if they could pick out the man who came to the station. These witnesses included the constable who made the report. The other witnesses were too frightened to pick out anyone at the identification parade, but the constable straight away identified Corporal Pritchard.

Both Pritchard and Robinson were on deputation from the regiment which lost the money. Pritchard was again questioned by me, this time in the presence of the Adjutant. Pritchard was a very fine Rugby football player, as was the Adjutant, and the latter had a special influence over him because of this. At the Adjutant's insistence, Pritchard agreed to help by making a statement. So I asked him:

> "What were you doing at that Railway station at that time of night?"
>
> "Well, Sir, I went to find the 'treasure'."
>
> "Oh, indeed and what made you go to the camp to find the 'treasure'?"
>
> "I had come to know that the 'treasure' was buried near the camp and I went to get it, intending to hand it over to the C.O.".
>
> "How did you come to know this and what information were you acting on?"

"It was like this", he said, "I was sitting one day in the regimental canteen having a drink alone. Three chaps were sitting at the next table and I overheard what they were talking about. They were talking about the 'treasure' and were drawing diagrams on bits of paper. One of the diagrams fell on the floor without their knowing it. When they left I picked it up. It was a diagram of the sand dunes opposite the camp, and from what was drawn on it I formed an idea as to where the 'treasure' was buried. Unfortunately when I came to know that you were on to my having gone out there, I threw the diagram away".

I did not question his veracity at the time. The false signature on the cycle register was enough to show that Pritchard's part in the affair was not altogether innocent, but to have shown that I thought he was lying would probably have dried up this source of information too quickly. I said:

> "What about the second cycle you hired? If you went out alone why did you want two cycles?"
>
> "Well, Sir, I did not like the idea of going all that way alone, so I persuaded Cpl Robinson to go with me."
>
> "What happened to Robinson that he did not come back with you?"
>
> "We started out together all right but as were going along,

talking and joking, we bumped into each other and Robinson's front wheel got buckled. He couldn't go on, so it was arranged that he would go back and that I would go on and pick up the 'treasure'."

"Then what happened when you got to the camp?"

"Believe it or not", he said, "But when I got there I got the jitters and funked even looking in the sand dunes. I rode to the railway station as fast as I could and took the first train back. What really scared me was the loneliness of the place and when the jackals and foxes started to call out their weird cries. I couldn't face it, and bolted."

I was very much inclined not to believe this story. If his motives had been clean he would have informed his officers of the story of the diagrams. His failure to do so could hardly be put down to a desire to delay giving this information until he had brought off the coup of finding and delivering the treasure. I was, in fact, inclined at first to believe that he might have found the money and brought it in, keeping quiet about this. I decided to leave this aspect to be tested later by keeping a watch on him. I did, however, test him by one more crucial question. Would he answer truthfully?

"Who were the three chaps you heard discussing the treasure in the canteen?"

After some hesitation he came out with the names:

"They were", he said, "Privates Brooks, Jones and Brown of our Battalion".

I was delighted to have this statement, for two of these men were the two who had exchanged remarks about the dictaphone when passing each other at the time of the general interrogation of the battalion. I left it at that and did not question Pritchard any more for the time being, but turned my attention to Corporal Robinson. This man was at first rather sulky. After the identification parade at which he was picked out by the cycle dealer, he could hardly deny his share in that transaction. He admitted having hired two cycles with Pritchard, and having gone along, the road, and having the collision, but he maintained that he knew nothing more as to the object of the journey.

Meanwhile reference to the local police revealed further corroboration of the story of the cycle collision. It so happened that, in connection with the operation against the criminal tribe of dacoits already mentioned, a ring of police had been placed round the town and cantonments. One of these pickets was stationed on the metalled road leading out of the camp. Inquiry from this picket revealed an entry in their diary that a European in mufti, believed to be a 'gora', had passed through the picket *on foot* late at night, about eleven o'clock.

I connected this with the story given out by Pritchard and Robinson, and made a rough calculation of the distance that the two must have travelled in the time. I then decided to try to get Robinson to help me find the cycle which was missing. At that time of year there was still a good deal of the Kharif crop (winter crop) still standing in the field, and I thought it probable that Robinson might have hidden the cycle somewhere in the crops at the side of the road. So I took him along with me in my motorcycle and sidecar on this road, and stopped when we had come to the point which I thought they might have reached. It so happened that there were no crops standing at this point, but there was a village pond on one side of the road. It suddenly struck, me that perhaps he had thrown the cycle into this pond. So I said to him:

> "Here we are! You must have collided with Pritchard somewhere about here, and I believe you chucked the cycle in this pond.
>
> "You're very clever, Mister", he said "but you're not quite right. After Pritchard had gone on, and I had started to go back, when I had gone about a mile, I got fed up with pushing the cycle along with a buckled wheel. It was an awful sweat pushing it, so I did chuck it in a pond, not this one but the one we have already passed down the road".

So we went back and found a larger pond, sure enough about a mile back. It was quite deep and the area of water had been much swollen by some recent rain. I collected some men from the village nearby. We started a sort of dragging operation in the pond, and, after some time, came across the cycle, which was duly retrieved from the water.

Robinson now changed his tune. He admitted his share in the effort to recover the money. The circumstances of the recovery of the cycle had made him come to think I knew all about the whole affair, and he himself volunteered the information that Pritchard had not been on the level and had only told half the story.

So Corporal Pritchard was again questioned, and this time he was induced to come clean. The story of picking up the diagram in the canteen he now admitted was false. Actually Brooks, Jones and Brown had negotiated with him to proceed to the camp and bring back the money which they said they had buried in a jackal's hole in the sand dunes. They had forgotten the topography of the place, and merely told him that the hole was about four hundred yards from the road. He had, however, as he thought, a pretty good idea where to look, and he and Robinson had set out with every hope of success.

It was apparently true that Pritchard had lost his nerve. A moonlight night had been purposely chosen for the journey, so as to enable them to see where to look; this only served to enhance the eeriness of the place when he got there. It was a wild spot, right out in the open jungle, and not far off a big river flowed by with deep cavernous ravines on its banks. There were, it is true, no tigers or leopards about, but jackals and foxes made the night hideous with their calls, and the palm trees threw long shadows on the sand dunes. There was no habitation within miles, except the wayside railway station, the lights of which were exceedingly welcome to him. He never plucked up courage to stay on the spot and look round. He cycled through the Jungle as fast as he could to the railway station and, of course, came back without the 'treasure'. It was in no spirit of loyalty to the regiment, or of public duty that he had undertaken the journey. He and Robinson had been let into the conspiracy as accessories after the fact. We have already seen how an effort had been made to get hold of a motor car. This having failed, the next best thing was cycles, as the railway might be watched. The chief conspirators had no hope of getting out of the cantonments for long enough, so they had to enlist the confidence and assistance of someone who was in a position to go out. For this reason they had sought out the two corporals of the regiment who were employed in the Brigade Office.

The Statements of these two corporals were sufficient to make us renew our attentions to the men who had already come under suspicion, Jones and Brown, and the new man, Brooks. At once a very significant fact came to light, namely that *Brooks had been in the Headquarters Guard on the night of the occurrence and had been on sentry-go from midnight till two o'clock in the morning.*

Inquiry from the Company Commander elicited the fact that this man was always very smartly turned out. There was a custom in the unit that those who were for guard duty in the next twenty-four hours were paraded before the Orderly Officer, and the smartest man was 'given the stick'. This meant that he was excused Guard duty and had the sinecure job of doing orderly to the C.O. next day. In the past, Brooks had almost invariably been selected for 'stick orderly' and so evaded guard duty. On this occasion, his buttons were not properly polished. Obviously this was intentional and he duly did duty in the guard on the night in question, which was clearly what he had planned.

Having ascertained this much, I managed to get the C.O. to agree to the three men being taken into custody and kept in separate cells. I then proceeded to try to reconstruct the crime, and in the light of that reconstruction, to see what I could get out of the suspected persons themselves. I adopted a method of auto-suggestion which – in its perverted form, is known as 'the third degree'. It is one thing to induce a person to make a statement by putting him in fear, or by questioning him in a manner which really amounts to violence, but it is quite another to induce the suspect to tell you what he knows by making it appear to him that you know it already. On the contrary, he is encouraged by suggestion to volunteer the required information. Hence the coining of the term 'auto-suggestion'. There is nothing in the least immoral or improper in such a method, and it is a method which, in the hands of a patient investigator, produces results which perhaps would not be achieved by other means.

Daily questioning of these men helped progressively to reconstruct the crime and at the same time, to convince them that I knew all about it, and they became more and more forthcoming. This applied, however, only to Jones and Brown, especially the former. It proved of no avail with Brooks. As I learnt afterwards, he was too hardened a criminal to react. He was clearly the master crook behind the whole affair, and he was just saying nothing.

Jones and Brown were, however, newcomers to crime, and were gradually worn down by patient interrogation, spread over ten days or more. I was sure that these men were thieves, and I was gradually converting the Officers of the battalion to this view. They started to co-operate and be helpful. The attitude of the officers reacted on the rank and file, and evidence, previously suppressed, was now tendered. Further interrogation, in particular, of the personnel of the guards brought out at last one piece of corroborative evidence. Consequently the innocent among them, and they were all innocent except Brooks, now started to ensure that they were cleared of suspicion.

But if there was one person in the headquarters guard who was guilty, did this also indicate that there was a guilty person in the adjoining guard; that of A. Coy? I checked up the time each man in the two guards was on sentry-go. The important point was clearly – who was on sentry-go at the same time as Brooks? Was he an accomplice? If not, how did Brooks get over his presence on guard over the next tent? Previously the N.C.O. in charge of both guards had stoutly denied that anything had occurred which would have had any bearing on the case. On being questioned now, however, the corporal in charge of A. Coy guard stated that sometime after midnight on Friday night he had found the man who should have been on sentry-go in his bed, and he had sent him off back to his post. This man, a lad still in his teens, now stated that soon after midnight, when he was on sentry-go and Brooks was on duty at the Headquarters guard, Brooks had told him he would look after both posts so that he, the young recruit, could go to sleep, which he did, and was duly caught by the corporal and sent back. That was how Brooks got over the presence of the other sentry.

So now we had the following points clear –

(1) That Brooks was on duty at the Headquarters guard tent from twelve midnight to two o'clock.
(2) That he secured the absence of the other sentry by persuading him to go off to bed.
(3) That he was friendly with Jones and Brown.
(4) That Brooks, Jones and Brown had conspired with Pritchard and Robinson to go and fetch the money.
(5) That someone had previously tried to get a car out of the proprietor of the restaurant clearly for some purpose.
(6) That the money had not been found with anybody in the unit.
(7) That enough had been divulged to Pritchard and Robinson to indicate that the money had been buried somewhere in the sand dunes.

The obvious deductions from the above facts indicated that while Brooks was on sentry-go, Jones and Brown had come along and Brooks, had handed them the strong-box, which they had carried over to the opposite side of the road and emptied it of notes and cash which they had hidden somewhere. The restaurant proprietor now agreed that he could identify the soldier who had approached him for the car. At an identification parade he picked Brooks, thus carrying the evidence against the gang a step further. But there was still quite insufficient to go on to put them in court. None of the money had been recovered; practically all the incriminating evidence against them was circumstantial. It was true Jones and Brown, Pritchard and Robinson had all made statements to me, but the Law of Evidence in India does not permit of statements made by accused or suspected persons to a police officer being used as evidence against them. Evidence could have been given of the statement which led to the recovery of the cycle, and the evidence of Pritchard and Robinson could he used if they were not co-accused. But we really could not say how far they were in the original conspiracy, and we still wanted something substantial to build up our case. In particular, we wanted to recover the money. It was now clear that we must rely on assistance from the main conspirators for this purpose. By this time I thought that Jones had been sufficiently worked upon for an experiment to be tried. I arranged to take him out to the camp. He was to travel the sixty miles in a military lorry on another moonlight night. No-one was to talk to him on the way. In the lorry was a military escort and a civil police sergeant. I followed in my car with the C.O. and the Adjutant.

Thinking things over, I decided in my mind that there must be some landmark which they had fixed in their minds to guide them when they came back to lift the money. If they had buried it in the sand dunes, the spot would be difficult to identify without such a mark, or without a prolonged search. When we got to the camp, I surveyed the area from the road. By chance there was a lone palm tree. I thought this might be their landmark. So I called up Jones and said, "That lone palm tree must be the mark which you had in mind to guide you if you came back to get the money. What about it"?

Without further demur, he said "No, not that one, but I'll show you one on the other side".

So he took us right round the sand dunes, and there, on the other side, was another lone palm tree. Under it was a large jackal's hole.

"That's where we buried the money" he said, and promptly knelt down, and put his hand down the hole and brought out bundle after bundle of notes! Actually this lot amounted to Rs 44,000.

"Now", he said, "I have to measure two arms lengths, and we shall find an earthenware pot in the ground, with the rest of the money in it".

Suiting the action to the word, he measured two arms lengths, scratched away in the sand with his fingers and found – nothing! But there was a round shaped hole where the earthenware pot had clearly been. Jones turned round from where he was kneeling on the ground, and said to the C.O. "That detective bloke has got the rest"!

Our auto-suggestion talks had convinced him that I knew all about it, and where the money had been buried, and had taken my share!!

Anyhow, the reward of so many weeks investigation was the

recovery of half the stolen property. But I was not satisfied with that. What had happened to the rest? Had our friend Corporal Pritchard double-crossed us after all? Had he actually found the place of burial, hit upon half the treasure in the pot, and made off, keeping the find to himself? Somehow I did not think he had the guts to do even this much and get away with it.

But someone must have found the pot and carried off the money. If anyone with knowledge had come to the spot, and found the pot, why could not he have found the notes in the jackal's hole, which was much easier? It seemed to me probable that someone had accidentally come across the earthenware pot, and found that part of the 'treasure', without knowing that there was more money in the jackal's hole.

A few weeks after finding the money, a note of one hundred rupees of the missing series, was impounded in a grog shop across the river. This set all my doubts, at rest, and was proof positive that the rest of the notes were in the locality. So we continued to watch – slender though the hope seemed to be of coming on to the persons who made this find, by what must have been an accident.

The camp was situated about two miles from an opium Department Depot. Opium production was then allowed. When the opium crop was ready, the cultivators used to bring in their crude opium for sale to the Department who paid in currency notes. Village bankers used to attend the camp and cash the notes for the cultivators at a discount. The season for these transactions had now arrived, and it seemed not improbable that an attempt would be made to unload the stolen notes en masse at this opportunity. So constables were sent in plain clothes to keep a lookout for this possibility. Luck was again on our side. One of these constables came to know of a transaction between two bankers and some Chamars (low caste Hindus) of the locality. He went along and actually witnessed the handing over of Rs 30,000 in 2,000 Rs notes. As soon as the transaction was complete, the banias (bankers) got on to an ekka (one-horse trap) which they had with them, and made off. The constable followed in another ekka knowing that they would have to pass a police station in a small town some five miles off. He planned to catch up with them at this police station, and actually succeeded in catching up with them there. He jumped out of his ekka and took the two banias into the police station and put them before the officer-in-charge, saying that they had got the notes on them. The banias were searched, but much to the astonishment and chagrin of the constable, nothing was found on them. The constable had the sense to realise what had happened. They must have passed the notes to the driver of the ekka. He rushed out only to find that the driver had driven off. The banias must have realised that they were being followed.

The constable mounted his ekka, came straight to Headquarters to me and told his story. The first ekka must have had a good start and not been caught up in the ten mile distance between the other town and headquarters. Rapid inquiry was made and the city police succeeded in ascertaining the identity of the ekka driver. A visit to his home showed that he had come back, stabled his horse and trap and then gone off again. It was conjectured that he would go to the railway station (there was no bus or lorry transport in those days) and make for some distant spot. The town was only a medium sized one and the railway station did not have much traffic. It was easy to check the tickets. There was only one third-class ticket taken for a long distance, and that was for Bombay. A sub-inspector and the constable who could, of course, now identify the driver, went off by the first train. At the junction they caught the mail train which passed the slow train in which the ekka driver was travelling. When the slow train drew up at the Byculla terminus in Bombay, he got out, little suspecting that he had been followed, and was picked up at the barrier. On his person were found nearly Rs 30,000 in notes of the series stolen from the battalion!

Thus about Rs 75,000 of the stolen Rs 90,000 was recovered. The balance represented the amount which the Chamars had succeeded in passing off in the locality and which they had spent on 'wine, women and song'. Inquiries showed that these Chamars, when collecting grass from the sand dunes for the village cattle, had actually struck the earthenware pot with the khurpa (a small instrument used for cutting grass). On breaking the pot they found what to them was untold wealth, Rs 46,000 in notes. They must have realised that this was part of the money which had been stolen from the regiment because the story of that theft had been broadcast in all the surrounding villages. They did not inform the police but buried the notes in the walls of their houses until they thought it safe to use them. Then the inquiry which followed the impounding of the note at the grog shop across the river made them frightened, and they decided to unload the remainder at the time of the opium sales. Thus their accidental find cost them, in the end, their freedom for six months.

Meanwhile the original gang of three private soldiers were sent up for trial. On conviction they were sentenced to a long term of imprisonment. Jones and Brown confessed, but Brooks continued to maintain that he had been framed by 'that detective bloke'. He got two years more than the other two.

Further inquiries from England revealed that he was a previous convict who had served a sentence for breaking into an English cathedral and stealing some gold plate. He was, in fact, a known gangster and master-crook, who had been overlooked during World War 1.

Thus was proved in the end, the correctness of the theory that the crime itself cannot lie. The facts of every case indicate in varying degrees the quarter in which the culprit should be sought. This crime could only have been committed by those who had the chance to know that the opportunity was there, and that the opportunity was to be short lived. Outsiders could not have had the knowledge, and the facts clearly showed 'ab initio' that it was an inside job. One can appreciate the C.O's anxiety to preserve the name of his regiment, and his reluctance to face the facts, but the indications were there from the start.

IT MIGHT HAVE BEEN DIFFERENT

I had ridden over to a village about six miles from the mango grove where my tents were pitched in almost the most inaccessible part of the district. I had managed to get my car there by using canal bank roads which were not open to the public. It was with considerable surprise, therefore, that on my return in the dusk, I saw two men, obviously townspeople, standing, near the grove.

As I drew near I thought I recognised one of the prominent Congress workers of the city, a man who, though one of the national leaders of the anti-government agitation, I knew to be of stirling character and a selfless patriot. I had come into close personal touch with him over an affair in which he had become involved. Information had been laid with the police that a live bomb was being kept on the premises which housed the printing press from which he made his living. A search warrant had been obtained from the Magistrate who, however, had laid down that the warrant should be executed in the presence of a high police official. So I decided to go myself. The bomb was duly discovered, but in circumstances which convinced me that it had been planted. Nevertheless the bomb had been recovered from his premises and he could have been held responsible, so his arrest and detention in jail would have been perfectly justified. In spite, however, of the insistence of the city police chiefs, I had refused to allow his arrest. I suppose that my sympathetic attitude on this occasion had given him the impression that I was not the uncompromising hard-faced police official I was generally supposed to be.

During the investigation I had occasion to have long discussions with him, not only about the reasons which led to the planting of the bomb, but on the affairs of the country generally. I came to get a much better insight into the motives which were actuating many of the men who were taking part in the agitation against the Government of India and the British administration. I came to realise how genuine and sincere were his own personal motives and to appreciate how deeply he was involved in the general conspiracy to overthrow the Government and secure independence for the country. I found that he was fully acquainted with the general and detailed plans of the movement. He took good care not to give away anything which might enable preventive action to be taken against particular persons. He avoided mentioning any names and was careful not to give away the whereabouts of any workers who had disappeared and gone underground. He was in the movement solely from patriotic motives. He was a declared and devoted disciple of the great leader of the movement, Mahatma Gandhi. He was convinced of the necessity of keeping the two great religious communities of India, Hindus and Muslims, together, and he devoted himself to the cause of Hindu-Muslim unity. Indeed, so strongly was this motive imbued in him that he subsequently became a martyr to this cause and gave his life in an attempt to stem a huge communal conflagration which occurred a few years later. He fell a victim to the insensate fury of a Muslim mob when he left the safety of his own locality to go into Muslim localities to try to persuade them to agree to stop the senseless communal fighting that had been going on for about a week.

It was this gentleman whom I found waiting for my return, dressed in the nationalist garb (spotless white homespun cloth known as khaddar) with a white Gandhi cap on his head. His companion was a sort of servant or bodyguard. The pair had come by train to the railway station, and hiring a bullock cart from a nearby village, had come across the ten miles to my camp.

As I came cantering in towards the grove, the Pandit held up his hand, and signalled me to stop. It was only then that I really recognised who he was.

"Halloa. Panditji, I said. "What brings you out here all this way"?

"Sahib, I want to see you alone most urgently. I have purposely come at dusk so that I could be sure no one would recognise me when I approached your camp. I did not want anyone to know, particularly the local police. I have accosted you like this on the road, so that I would not have to get myself announced to you by your orderlies. Where can I see you alone and at once?

I dismounted and handed my horse to my syce (groom), and suggested to the Pandit that we walked down the canal bank, where we could talk as we walked along. The canal road was always little frequented, and by nightfall was absolutely deserted. There was no fear of our conversation being overheard, or the identity of my companion being revealed.

Before relating what he had to say, I must recapitulate briefly some of the facts of the Indian political situation as it was in those days. It was the period of the second great non-co-operation movement started by Mahatma Gandhi. From the time of the first World War, there had been a great surge forward of the movement for the independence of India. In the years immediately after the 1914-18 War there had been, amongst others, the Khilafat agitation, and the near-rebellion in the Punjab. The campaign was brought to an end by the Mahatma himself after the incident at Chauri Chaura in the Gorakhpur district of the United Provinces. A mob attacked a police station and burnt it down. Many of its police inmates perished in the flames or were brutally murdered. Mahatma Gandhi then confessed he had committed a Himalayan blunder, and called off the movement.

For some years overt agitation died down until the Mahatma again initiated the agitation which came to be known as the Civil Disobedience movement. The idea was that the Government would be brought to its knees and the administration paralysed if the people could be induced to withdraw co-operation with the Government in the day to day administration. In particular, taxes were not to be paid; people would refrain from seeking redress in the law courts; members of the Bar would refrain from pleading; use would not be made of police stations and people would settle their own quarrels and disputes. It was even contemplated setting up a parallel administration which would administer justice locally. The movement duly started with the march of the Mahatma to the sea to make salt illegally. This was because the immediate and ostensible cause of the rising was the doubling of the Salt Tax needed to balance the Budget of the central Government. Although the movement actually failed, a great deal of dislocation occurred and considerable harm was being done to the country's trade and prosperity. Congress circles themselves came to realise that it was a mistake and a costly failure. On the other hand Government felt it to be a serious embarrassment which it was essential to bring to a peaceful end. Accordingly both sides were willing to compromise and open negotiations for a settlement.

It is unnecessary to follow the history of those negotiations, which included the calling of the Round Table Conference in London. We are only concerned with that part of the negotiations which involved a personal meeting between the Viceroy and the Mahatma. The extremists and hot-heads of the Congress were by no means pleased with the turn of events. They wanted a definite, even a violent, showdown, and the idea of negotiations which might lead to a peaceful and friendly settlement was highly distasteful to them. This would only lead to the ultimate grant of Dominion Status, and probably leave India within the orb of the British Empire. They wanted something far more dynamic; something revolutionary which would bring about an immediate and complete severance from Britain. So this section of Congress was determined to do all in its power to prevent negotiations from starting, and, in particular, to prevent the meeting of the Viceroy and Mahatma Gandhi. It was at this stage that the journey of the Pandit to my camp took place.

As soon as we were definitely out of earshot of the people in my camp, he opened the conversation. "Sahib, I have come to you because at the time of the discovery of the bomb at my press, you showed me some sympathy. I believe you will appreciate my position, and will deal with the information which I have come to impart to you in a manner which will enable me to keep the confidence of my fellow-workers, and at the same time avoid an awful catastrophe. I cannot possibly face it being revealed that it is I who have given you this information. I am therefore asking you to assure me that you will take no action against me, or any action which will result in it being known that I gave you the information. I give you my solemn word that I have not committed any criminal act, nor joined in any conspiracy to do so. Now, Sahib, will you give me your promise"?

I had no idea what sort of information he was going to give me. I thought it must be some local crime that had occurred or some miscarriage of justice about to be perpetrated by our wrong action in some local case of murder, and that this was the catastrophe to be avoided. In view of what I knew about the Pandit's connection with the extremists, it did actually enter my head that possibly the information did concern some political crime, but of a local nature. I believed his assurance that he was not criminally involved, and I saw no harm in giving him the assurance he asked for. But I was not prepared for the nature of the information which he now proceeded to give me, nor for its importance and urgency.

"I am giving you this information" he went on, "chiefly because I am an implicit believer in our Master's policy of non-violence. Like him, I cannot countenance any act of violence against any human being, even against my enemies. As you well know, I am in with the hot-heads of our party, and I have come to know a great deal about their plans. As long as these plans have not involved direct violence, I have gone along with them. But now I have come to know of a definite plan to use violence. I have come to know that they are planning an attempt on the Viceroy's life. In fact, I have learnt that there are some among them who are incensed with the possibility of The Mahatma 'selling the pass' and coming to terms with the Viceroy. So they have concocted a plan which, if successful, would probably cause the death of the Viceroy and the Mahatma together. I have not been able to ascertain actual details but I conjecture that there will be an attempt to prevent the meeting of the two. I rather think that they intend somehow to explode a bomb when the Viceregal party arrives at Delhi".

The gravity of this information momentarily stunned my mind. When I recovered from the shock of it, I realised the imperative necessity of doing something about it immediately. *The special train was to reach Delhi early next day.* Unfortunately, as the route to be taken did not pass through my district, I had not been given information of the timings of the journey.

But how was I to convey to the authorities at Delhi the purport of the terribly significant information just given me? Here was I, in the most inaccessible part of my district, miles from any means of telephonic or even telegraphic communication. Moreover what was I going to tell them, especially in a telephonic message which would have to be in code? My friend had not told me of any detailed plot. He had not given me enough information to conjecture where the attempt would be made. It might be made at the point of departure. It might be made anywhere on the route. In either of these cases it might have already taken place. I knew, of course, that stringent precautions would have been made all along the railway, and particularly at Delhi station, and there was no possibility of anything being achieved at the Viceroy's House. It could, however, be attempted on the road journey from the station to the House. From every point of view I must somehow get the information first to Delhi. I must take the risk involved in cutting out the proper channel of communication through my own superiors at provincial headquarters.

But I must make further efforts to try to get something tangible out of him, at least as to the nature of the attempt that was to be made, if not the exact locality. But either he did not know, or because he was not prepared to divulge any information which might lead to the revelation of the identity of the persons involved in the conspiracy, he maintained his denial that he knew any further details.

"From what, I can gather, Sahib", he said, "they have a definite plan to compass the death of the Viceroy. How, when and where I do not know, except that the whole idea is to prevent His Excellency and the Mahatma meeting. The attempt is going to be made in the very early future, indeed in the next twenty-four hours".

There was clearly nothing to be gained from further cross-examination of the Pandit. I must get on with the business of planning how to get the information to the authorities. My only chance was centred on the fact that I had my car with me. I thought of the idea of motoring back straight away to my Headquarters, from where I could get into telephonic, or at least telegraphic, communication with Delhi.

Meanwhile I could not leave the Pandit and his companion there in the jungle at that time of night, nor could I take him into my camp where his identity would become revealed to the various members of the local police who would be on duty there. So I arranged that he would stay on the canal bank, and that I would pick him up in my car and take him along with me to the wayside railway station where he had alighted.

I left him and walked towards my camp. On the way I recollected that I had insufficient petrol to take me to Headquarters. I was expecting a fresh supply to be brought out with my correspondence next day, but, of course, I could not wait for that, and I had to think again. It so happened that the Headquarters town of the neighbouring district was closer to my camp than my own headquarters, and I reckoned I could just make that town on the petrol I had left. From there I would be able to get in touch by telegram with Delhi.

So after making a hasty meal and bidding farewell to my wife, whom I had to leave there with my entourage, right out in the jungle, I started off down the canal bank road accompanied by two orderlies. We picked up the Pandit and his servant, and made for the town which could be reached by a metalled road which joined the canal road about twenty miles down. We reached the outskirts of the town without incident, when Panditji announced he could not risk going through the town, even at that early hour of the morning. He was well known to the inhabitants and to the local police. He asked to be put down, and said he would find his way to a small station and catch a train.

I went into the town which was not, in those days, connected with the long distance telephone system. I tried to get in touch with the Chief of Police in Delhi through the railway control telephone, but failed. I had to sit down and encode a cipher telegram setting out the gist of my information. Subsequently I ascertained that this message was delayed in delivery. However, I decided I would go on to Delhi to hand over personally the information I had been given. I drove to Agra where I obtained details of the timing of the Viceroy's special train. It was to reach Delhi in about three hours time or less. I took the road to Delhi which went along the west side of the river Jumna because it had a good surface and ran quite close to the railway line along which the Viceregal train was travelling. Owing to some trouble which I had with my car, I reached the point in the road just about the same time as the special train. As it roared past I heaved a sigh of relief. Apparently nothing untoward had happened. I could see at various points on the line the police on duty to guard the permanent way, and the end of the journey was almost in sight.

Some distance further on, the line leaves the road to pass over wild country, everywhere intersected by ravines leading down to the Jumna. There was no human habitation whatsoever in the area. The train came racing over this last stretch of the journey. The staff must have been thinking of getting ready for the arrival at the terminus. Suddenly there was a terrific explosion which must have shaken the train from end to end, and could be heard for miles around.

Then did I realise what the plan of the conspirators had been, and that it had now been put into operation. I imagined that the whole train must have been wrecked, that, in fact, the plot had succeeded; that the Viceroy would almost certainly be among the casualties, for the train must assuredly have been derailed and toppled over into the ravine on either side of the line. I began to consider how far I must hold myself responsible for this awful result, to reproach myself for not having been able to get the information about the intended plot in time to the higher authorities. My self-condemnation was quite unreasonable, for my information was vague in the extreme and only given to me at the last moment. But still I could not get away from the idea that foreknowledge of the event was in my possession and criminal intelligence was my area of responsibility. Really efficient intelligence work should have revealed to me the existence of persons in my area who at least knew about the conspiracy to murder the Viceroy. I worked myself into a real stew over the matter and had begun seriously to worry over what action which I should now take.

But, in fact, there was no need for all this self-examination of responsibility or for self-condemnation. For a miracle had occurred. The train almost completely survived the explosion and steamed on to the journey's end, those travelling in it blissfully ignorant of what had occurred. Subsequent examination showed that somehow the conspirators had managed to mine the railway track and place explosive under the line. By great good fortune, however, only one side of the line blew up and although a considerable gap was caused on this side of the rails, the whole train passed over it. A large piece of rail did, however, strike the underpart of that part of the special train which formed the dining car. The only person in this compartment was an unfortunate Indian servant, who was mortally injured by the impact.

The incident had occurred some distance from the road. It was not my place to proceed to the scene to investigate the cause of the explosion. I went on into Delhi, and later made contact with the local senior police officers, from whom I learnt of the escape of the Viceroy and his whole party in the train. The outcome was a comparatively minor tragedy. But had the plot succeeded to the full, the result would been very different. A complete catastrophe might have occurred which would have had a very profound effect on the relations between the British and India, and might well have altered the whole of subsequent Indian history. I would then have had some real cause for bemoaning the fact that I had not been able to get through with my information and avert a really great tragedy.

Yes, the outcome might have been very different.

THE PERFECT CRIME

Many writers of detective fiction have set out to describe 'the perfect crime'. This is a story of a perfect crime of real life. In one respect only does it resemble the perfect crime of fiction, namely, that the crime turned out not to be quite perfect, and the truth did 'out' in the end. In fiction this result is always achieved as the result of brilliant deduction by a master detective. In this case, the truth came out fortuitously, sheer bad luck as far as the criminal was concerned.

Although the adage 'truth is stranger than fiction' can be demonstrated to be an untruth or, only a half truth, in this case the actual facts were so much like fiction that the story does indeed appear to be an endeavour to describe the perfect crime. Partly in the interests of clarity, and partly because connections of the dramatis personae may still be alive, it is necessary to present some facts in a disguised form but the main facts constituting the crime are given as, they occurred. The names are, for the same reason, fictitious. The story is, however about one of the most remarkable crimes in Indian criminal history.

What are the features that constitute the perfect crime? I would suggest that, in the case of murder, they are:

(1) That there should be no eye-witness of the murder.
(2) That there must be left no trace of the murder.
(3) That there should be no accomplice who might give the show away.
(4) That there should appear to be no motive, or at least, no sufficient motive, for the murder.
(5) And finally, that the death should appear to be natural or accidental.

It is obvious that if these circumstances were all present in respect of an individual's death, it, would be difficult, well nigh impossible, to realise that a murder had occurred. There would be no necessity to look for a murderer, still less to bring anyone to justice for it. Even the writers of detective fiction never attempt to write a story of a murder of which the truth did not 'out' sooner or later. In real life, there are, of course, a number of murders which remain untraced, but the failure to solve these problems must always be due to the investigation not having been perfect. The perfect murder can ideally be answered by the perfect investigation. In this case, but for a fortuitous circumstance, the murder would never have been investigated and, further, luck again favoured the police investigation. The success of the investigation was in no way due to the brilliance of a Sherlock Holmes or a Poirot.

Some years ago, there lived in England a wealthy family. The owner of that wealth at the time of this story was a woman in her late twenties by the name of Garnet Orme. She was a religious-minded woman and a leader of the social and religious life of the village. She herself took a class in the Church Sunday School. In the same village lived a young man named Edward Grant. He was a great athlete and he, too, was religious minded, helping at the village Sunday School. The two families were well known to each other and a friendship grew up between them.

Grant joined the Indian Police and a few months' absence revealed to both of them that they were in love with each other. Miss Orme decided to go out to India, and after a short interval, the two friends got engaged.

Miss Orme wanted somebody to go out with her as a companion and advertised in the papers. Among the applicants was a Miss Wright who had been trained as a nurse and proved herself to be a highly entertaining personality. Miss Orme's health was not very good, and she engaged her at once. They went out to India together and went to live in Lucknow where Grant was stationed.

Some time after they arrived in India Grant unfortunately contracted enteric fever. In spite of the best medical attention and the professional services given him by Miss Wright, who attended to him with the utmost care and devotion, he died. This sad event proved a great shock to Miss Orme and she suffered a serious breakdown in health. Instead of returning to England, she stayed on in India in order to be near the grave of her beloved Edward. She visited the grave frequently and lived in a sort of dream, seeing visions of him. Miss Wright stayed on with her and, in fact, Miss Orme found she could not do without her companion. She felt very kindly disposed to her because of her devoted and voluntary effort to save young Grant's life by her ministrations as a nurse. Indeed, Miss Orme grew more and more attached to her. Her health at the same time became worse.

When the hot weather came round Miss Orme went up to the hills and took a suite of rooms in the best hotel of the hill station. Miss Wright went with her, but when the monsoon rains started, after about three weeks of it, she said she found the climate oppressive, and obtained her employer's permission to return to the plains for a month. She had been gone about fifteen days when Miss Orme became ill suddenly and died during the night. A private medical practitioner, a Dr Osborne, had been attending her off and on during her stay. He was called, and in due course gave the necessary certificate that she had died a natural death. Miss Wright w s summoned from the plains and made all the funeral arrangements. Miss Orme was duly buried.

These are the facts of the perfect crime. There was no eye-witness to any foul play; no accomplice to give the show away; no trace of any crime; and there appeared to be nobody with any motive for causing the death of the deceased lady. The doctor had certified that the death was natural. In fact there appeared to be no murder; no crime at all. There was thus all the ingredients of 'the perfect crime'.

Indeed the position would have remained but for a fortuitous circumstance unconnected with the criminal. The doctor who had certified natural death, though not a drunkard, was addicted to taking a good deal of liquor on convivial occasions. On the night on which he had been summoned to the hotel, he had been attending a good party, and had been indulging freely in the good things provided to eat and drink.

The doctor had a personal servant, a bearer or valet, a very smart and handsome young man. He had frequently visited the hotel where Miss Orme was staying, and had become intimate with her ayah or personal maid servant. Here comes in that rather amazing feature of Indian life, the bazaar rumour. Only those who have spent a lifetime in India can appreciate the frequency and accuracy with which the bazaar (which in this connection, means gossips of the local lower world) comes to know of matters which are hidden even from those who *should* know them. One frequently heard from subordinates or private servants, of matters or events which one thought were dead secret. The bazaar, moreover, frequently foretells events which occur in the future. It frequently gets hold, in some mysterious way, of the correct state of affairs.

In this case bazaar rumour had got to work about the death of Miss Orme. How it started, it is impossible to say. The existence of this rumour came to light in a peculiar way. An anonymous letter was received by the Editor of the local English Weekly Paper. It read in 'pidgin' English as follows:

> *The doctor who attended English lady dying in hotel very bad man . . . too much drink taken . . . not knowing true facts . . . a smell comes out of affair.*

The Editor promptly sent this communication to the local police headquarters. Although this did not amount to much, it was so unlike the usual anonymous letter or petition that it was thought worth while having preliminary inquiries made, instead of consigning it, as normal, to the waste paper basket.

The place to start these inquiries was obviously the bazaar. Some ferreting about among the servant classes, particularly the hotel servants and their connections, did elicit the fact that the bazaar did think there had been foul play. It was duly discovered that the author of the anonymous letter was the doctor's bearer. This man, when tackled, admitted sending it but could give no further information. He was merely going on bazaar rumour and what his lady love, the ayah, had hinted at. He had a grudge with his master over his wages, and he had merely done what was so often done in India, sent an anonymous letter to someone vaguely

115

in authority, thinking that, in a circuitous fashion it might react against his master. Nevertheless it did seem worth while going on with the inquiry on the strength of this man's information. For some reason or other the bazaar had suspected that there was something fishy in the matter.

An application was accordingly made to the Magistrate for the body of Miss Orme to be exhumed. This was granted, and a post mortem followed the exhumation. Later, chemical analysis showed the presence of a special form of arsenical poison in the viscera. It was fortunate that the exhumation had been carried out so soon after burial, as traces of this particular form of poisoning, would have quickly disappeared.

It was now clear that a murder had been committed after all.

Who was the murderer? Prima facie, it must be somebody who had the opportunity to administer the poison; somebody who had frequent, if not daily, access to the deceased. It must be somebody who would have had the opportunity to procure the poison. It must be somebody who would know the effect of the poison, and finally, it must be somebody who would have some motive for compassing the death of Miss Orme.

Motives for murder are legion, though personal benefit is the governing motive more generally found. Unlike the murders of fiction, the number of persons to be considered as possibly responsible for the murder was small. It seemed that there were only three persons who had any connection with the matter, namely the doctor, his bearer and the ayah. Miss Wright, the only other person to be connected with the deceased, had been four hundred miles away for fifteen days before the death. It did not seem necessary to consider her.

The doctor was the obvious suspect. He it was who would have the best opportunity to administer the poison. He was the man who possibly had the opportunity to procure the poison, and he it was who must be presumed to know its effects and how to handle it. But what motive could he have? It was unlikely that he could benefit by Miss Orme's death. He might possibly have administered the poison by mistake, and having discovered his error, hidden, as he thought, all trace of it, and got out of his difficulty by giving a natural death certificate. For it was the contradiction between his certificate and the result of the chemical analysis which was the most damning evidence against him.

Moreover, expert medical opinion was that the poison had been given in small doses over a longish period, and that the final dose, in conjunction with the accumulated effect of the previous doses, had been fatal. Clearly the doctor could have administered poison of this nature, and in this way, provided he could get hold of it. This did not, it is true, fit in with the theory of a possible mistake, but the possibility could not be ignored. So the police decided to search his premises. No result; no sign of poison of the required nature was found. When confronted with the discrepancy between his certificate and the results of the post mortem and chemical analysis, the doctor frankly admitted his own carelessness. Miss Orme had been ailing for some time, and he had not been able to diagnose her case. Her sudden death did not altogether surprise him, and he therefore gave a natural death certificate without sufficient care and attention. Asked to account for the anonymous letter sent by his bearer, he admitted that there had been unpleasantness with the young man, but could not in any way account for the man having given out the vague allegation made in the letter.

The bearer was tackled next. As already stated, he admitted having sent the letter, but said that his allegation against his master was a pure shot in the dark. His girlfriend, the ayah, had spun a lot of stories, but he knew nothing to account for the death.

The ayah was the next suspect. She, at least, could have had the opportunity of administering the poison. She could have had a motive. Possibly her mistress had caught her out over something, a theft or other delinquency. She possibly could have been so incensed against her mistress as to bring about her death. But the question as to how she could have got hold of the poison, and how she could have had the knowledge to use it, remained unanswered. Her belongings were nevertheless searched, and this time something tangible was found, which gave an unexpected turn to the inquiry.

Among her clothes was found a letter sent to her mistress and written by Miss Wright. This was a most fulsome letter declaring the writer's love and affection for her patron. In the course of the letter appeared this sentence:

> *Darling, I hope you are taking your medicine regularly. I am sure it must be doing you good and that, you have been able to see your dear Edward and have had lovely talks with him. But you must go on taking the medicine just as I told you, and when you take the dose I have fixed for August the fifteenth, then you will have the heavenly joy of Edward coming to you and staying all, night. Oh my dear, I wish I could be with you the next day to see how radiantly joyful you will look after your meeting with him.*

Miss Orme had left this letter on a table in her bedroom, and apparently the ayah had inadvertently taken it away with some clothes. She could not read the letter and was quite unaware of its contents. She was an intelligent young woman for her status, but quite illiterate. She volunteered the information that her mistress had been taking medicine prescribed by Miss Wright for some time, and that this medicine, instead of making her better, always seemed to make her worse.

A new dark picture thus appeared. Miss Wright now definitely came into the picture. She had made a large circle of friends. She played tennis well and was a good dancer. Several persons connected with the inquiry knew her well. They knew that Miss Orme thought the world of her, and was devoted to her. The fact, as disclosed in the will, that Miss Orme had left the bulk of her money to her did not, at first, seem at all significant, but now her position assumed a most sinister appearance, and the possibility of her having committed the murder inevitably came to be sifted.

Some strange circumstances came to light as a result of inquiries among the Europeans in the plains where they had lived in the cold weather. First, a peculiar remark made by her when she received a telegram from the hotel manager telling her of the death of her employer. She was playing tennis at the time. The young man who was her partner disclosed that she said before opening the telegram, "This must be about Garnet, but she could not have sent it herself".

Further enquiries led to several ladies of the station stating that Miss Wright appeared to have an extraordinary hold over the deceased. One lady, in particular, came forward to relate the following story which seemed to indicate that Miss Wright had indeed got the hold over her employer indicated in the letter found with the ayah.

This lady went to see Miss Orme one day at her bungalow, and found her solemnly turning over all the flower-pots round the house, and emptying their contents on the ground. The lady said to her:

"Garnet, what on earth are you doing?"

"Oh", said Miss Orme, "I have lost my engagement ring, and Marjorie says that if I turn over a hundred pots, one after the other, I shall find the ring in the hundredth".

She was duly carrying out this operation. The lady said:

"Why not go to the hundredth pot and turn it over?"

"No, that would not do, Marjorie says that would break the charm".

So she went on with the operation and, sure enough, when she turned over the hundredth pot, out tumbled the ring!

What had happened was clear. Obviously Miss Wright must have somehow got hold of the ring and placed it in that particular pot, and persuaded Miss Orme that if she turned them over, one after another, she would find the ring in the hundredth. This affair showed clearly that Miss Wright had obtained a hold over Miss Orme. The memory of her dear departed betrothed was so important to her, and the ring so precious, that she was frantic at its loss and was literally ready to leave no stone unturned in an endeavour to recover it.

The success of this subterfuge naturally made the hold which Miss Wright had achieved even stronger, and prepared the way for the scheme of getting the patient to take doses of medicines instructed, even in the absence of Miss Wright. So strongly had Miss Orme become imbued with the idea that the taking of potions prescribed by Miss Wright would lead to her meeting her dear departed one that she took the fatal dose.

Miss Wright was now examined. At first, with her usual sang-froid, she was able. to maintain a denial, but at length she was confronted with the letter found in the ayah's belongings. Her hand writing was so peculiar that she evidently thought that that it was no good denying that she had written the letter. Her self-possession melted away completely and she blurted out:

"I can't bear it any longer. I did it".

She then burst into tears and threw a genuine hysterical fit.

A search of her belongings disclosed one small article which was of great significance. A small empty envelope which was shown by later chemical analysis to contain particles of the same poison as that found in the viscera of the deceased. Later on, after the trial, it was discovered through inquiry in England that during the course of training to be a nurse she had had access to a store of poisonous drugs. It is an indication of her depraved character that she should have apparently taken possession of some drugs with the idea that she might use them later.

Actually, on receipt of the news of Miss Orme's death, Miss Wright had hastened to the hotel in the hills and removed all trace of her crime. There were probably other letters written during the fifteen days of her absence from her employer, which she had probably destroyed. She must have thought that the fatally significant letter found with the ayah had been destroyed by Miss Orme herself, and she never dreamt that that it had remained in the unwitting possession of the ayah.

Miss Wright thought that she had left no trace of her crime. She had no accomplice, although some suspected the complicity of the doctor whom she might have taken into her confidence, but there was no corroboration of this suspicion. She, in fact thought that she had succeeded in committing the 'perfect crime'. Seemingly she had, but fortune, as already related, had turned against her.

Later, however, the wheel of fortune turned in her favour. She was duly sent up for trial, and her case came before the High Court, as was the procedure in those days in the case of Europeans. The Leader of the local Bar, himself an Englishman, was engaged to defend her. The case against her rested entirely on circumstantial evidence, mainly on the finding of the letter which she had written, the finding among her belongings of the packet containing particles of poison and the evidence of the hold which which she had over Miss Orme when she was alive. The Law of Evidence precluded evidence being given of the statement made to the police.

The eminent lawyer who defended her made play of the fact that the accused was several hundred miles away when death occurred, and had been away for fifteen days. He played havoc in cross-examination with the highly strung ladies who spoke of the hold obtained by the accused over the deceased, and particularly with the lady who had to relate the story of the flower pots. The accused was acquitted.

Later, however, when Miss Wright went to him to take her case to prove probate of the will, which was disputed by a brother who came out from England, the lawyer said to her:

> "I was prepared to use my professional skill to get you off the charge of murder, but to help you enjoy the fruits of your crime, not on your life"!

He refused to take the case and she lost it. But in the end Fate overtook her. She disappeared from ken, and the First World War intervened. Some years later in England a certain doctor, who had an ailing wife, advertised for a nurse to help look after her. The person engaged was a Miss Howard, and she proved a very capable nurse. After some time she ingratiated herself with the doctor who fell in love with her. The two conspired to get rid of the ailing wife and she died. However, the circumstances were such as to arose suspicion and the police intervened. A post mortem was ordered and it was found that the lady had died of poisoning. Further inquiries showed first, that the poison used was the same as in the case of Miss Orme and, secondly, that Miss Howard was none other than Miss Wright.

This time there was no weakness of the law or of the evidence of which a clever lawyer could make play. She and the doctor were duly convicted and hanged.

It is perhaps idle, but interesting, to speculate whether Miss Wright had not in fact committed a third murder. Was the death of Edward Grant really due to enteric? Had she already committed 'the perfect crime'? and had this success been but a preliminary to an attempt to bring off another?

For Gallantry

In the main part of this book my father gave accounts of many dangers arising from his pursuit of criminals.

I now describe five deliberate attempts on his life. So many failed that the criminals came to believe that he had the power to turn bullets. The police came into possession of a letter from one of them in which the following appeared. "It is no use going for this Sahib, for he has a charmed life".

My father was awarded two King's Police medals and one Indian Police medal, all for gallantry.

A Butcher's Butchery

A certain master butcher had got himself into financial hot water and found himself going bankrupt. His financial worries had somewhat turned his brain and he hit upon the following scheme of dealing with his creditors. He invited them all round to his house on the pretext of arranging a settlement. He received them in the courtyard of his house where he was sitting, as it were in State to receive them, on a charpoy (string bamboo bed). Behind him he had concealed a double-barrelled sporting gun and a bag of cartridges. When the guests arrived, they removed their shoes and sat themselves on the ground in the yard. When they were all assembled and seated, he suddenly whipped out the gun and opened fire on them. Some of them managed to escape through the courtyard door, but several of them became casualties. The butcher then locked the door of his courtyard and got onto the flat roof of his house, from which point of vantage he proceeded to shoot off his gun, more or less aimlessly, but still highly dangerously. All the time he was uttering cries of defiance to the police and other authorities to come and arrest him.

My father happened to be staying at the house of the local Chief of Police, and the news of the affair was brought there. He thought it was up to him to deputise for the real incumbent, who was temporarily away, so he proceeded to the city with a young assistant. As the situation was not known to them and not properly reported, they both went down unarmed. On arrival at the scene they came to realise what was up. The situation was one which clearly demanded immediate action, if the madman was to be prevented from causing any more casualties. He proved even more defiant when he saw European officers had arrived. He danced up and down on his roof, brandishing his gun and occasionally firing it off, still apparently aimlessly.

My father decided to reconnoitre the place from the roof of the neighbouring houses, which operation was possible owing to the extra height of the adjoining houses. When he had managed to get himself in position to see the roof and courtyard of the butcher's house, he saw the butcher go down into his courtyard and lie on his charpoy with his gun. He also saw that a woman had come into the court yard from the interior of the house. She went to the door and took down the chain from the hasp. This had the effect of leaving the door so that it could be opened from the outside. As she was doing this the butcher shouted to her to come back, and actually levelled his gun at her. All this could be seen from the roof of the adjoining house, also the madman had laid his gun by his side on the bed *with the butt away from him.* My father decided to hasten down to the street accompanied by a small party and rush through the door. He intended to get to the butcher before he could use his gun, which was not now in the right position for a quick shot. Unfortunately in the few seconds taken by the party to get to the door, the butcher had changed the position of the gun. When the party, led by my father, burst into the courtyard he raised the gun and fired, but there was no report. My father slithered across the yard, which was covered with blood, and landed on top of the

124

madman, quickly overpowering him. In fact so heavily did he fall on him (he weighed nearly twenty stone) that the unfortunate man subsequently died in jail from the effects of being crushed. Subsequent examination of the gun revealed the reason for its failure. The butcher, in his haste, when he last loaded the gun had put in a spent cartridge. It was to this chance action of the madman that my father undoubtedly owed his escape.

Saved by a Dog

Later there was a period of intense overt underground agitation against the British Government. My father was in the very centre of the area involved, and became one of the targets of the terrorists. On no less than three occasions, attempts were made to get him. In the first of these cases it was the action of his dog, Tiger, which saved him.

Tiger was a ferocious-looking hound, a cross between a great Dane and a Rampur hound, a huge beast with an awe-inspiring bark and growl, but absolutely docile and unhostile. In the hot weather everyone slept out in the garden, as did my father, with Tiger tied to the foot of his bed. Within a yard or so of the bed was a clump of thick bushes. The very first night after Tiger's arrival, quite late on, the dog started to be restive and to pull at his chain. My father rather sleepily, without considering the reason for the dog's restiveness, let him loose, and turned over to go to sleep again. The dog thereupon growled furiously and leapt into the clump of bushes. From the other side of the bushes fled three men. Meanwhile, not realising what was happening, my father called the dog off and did not pursue the men. However the sentry, who was on guard at the back of the house, on hearing the dog's growls, had come round to the front and seen the men running off. They got clean away, but a search of the bushes revealed an evil-looking long knife and, perhaps more significantly, two masks of the Ku-Klux Klan pattern.

A vigorous check-up of suspicious characters followed. In one of the rooms of a local small hotel, police found a trunk which had been abandoned by its owner, who never returned to claim it. In it was a similar mask, and further investigation showed that some half-dozen persons had made a conspiracy to murder my father in his bed at night. Although they knew of the presence of the sentry, they thought they could creep up to the bed without being seen. The dog had only come that night, and they did not know about his presence, nor, of course, did they reckon on any interference from him. When he suddenly leapt into the bushes where they were stealthily creeping and let out his fierce growl, it was something they had not bargained for. He must have leapt on them as they were adjusting their masks, which they dropped with the knife and fled headlong. A near thing!

Thanks to the Sentry

Some time later, in the rainy season, my father was sleeping in the porch of his bungalow. Having learnt a lesson from the affair of the dog, he kept a revolver by his bed. On this occasion it was almost certainly only the fact that it was just midnight and time for a sentry change that saved him. He drowsily heard the sentry call "who goes there" in English, followed by a torrent of abuse in Hindustani. He then realised that something must be up and, leaping from his bed, he was just in time to see the sentry give chase down the drive. Seizing his revolver, he followed in haste. Two men had managed to get over the garden wall at a point just opposite my father's bed. The sentry's alertness prevented them from carrying out their nefarious plan of an attack on the bed. They ran off, followed by the sentry and my father who actually did get close enough to have a chance shot at the retreating miscreants. He did not think he could possibly have hit either of them, but next morning a pool of blood was found near the gate. The wounded man, however, was carried off by his comrades. Some time later it was discovered that this man was taken by train to a distant hospital where the bullet was extracted. He was one of the most dangerous of the terrorists who were working underground. He was subsequently arrested and hanged on a murder charge. But once more my father had escaped unhurt.

The Sadhu was a Bad Shot

Soon after, another attempt to get my father was made, and this time almost in daylight. Most evenings he used to spend at the Station Club, and the conspirators laid plans to shoot him as he entered the gates of the Club. He was driving the car himself, and in the back of the car was a 'shadow' orderly whose presence, however, proved no deterrent to the conspirator detailed to make the attempt. At the gate my father had to slow down the car. As he turned in, the man, in the saffron garb of a mendicant or Sadhu, came towards the car, as my father, thought to ask for alms. When practically on top of the car he whipped out a pistol and fired three shots, all of which hit the bodywork of the car and missed my father. The 'shadow' orderly returned the fire with his pistol, but in the failing light he could not be blamed for not hitting the false Sadhu, who fled away, discarding his long flowing robe. This time it was purely providential that a tragedy was averted.

A Lucky Silhouette

Later, it was again providence which brought about the most miraculous escape of all. This affair was not quite in cold blood, but in the course of operations to round up terrorists. A plan had been drawn up to draw into the net a number of terrorists who had collected in the town to assassinate a very high official. A large number of police officers had been collected, including my father. All had been given allotted tasks of going to various houses in the town and arresting conspirators believed to be staying in them. They had gone to the house where they had been informed that the leader of the gang was in hiding. They knew he had several fire-arms and suspected that he had some bombs as well. They thought he would be the man who would be the most likely to put up resistance and cause trouble, and took special precautions when surrounding and searching the house. However the terrorist surrendered without putting up a fight.

On the way back they heard shooting. My father got out of the car to go and investigate. He found a situation not unlike that of the master butcher. The police were searching a house where one of the lesser fry was believed to be. He was armed and had already fired at the sub-inspector who was sent to arrest him, wounding him in the stomach. Having done this he had gone to the roof of his house to try to escape, but could not get away as the police had been posted on the surrounding roofs, so he had come down to a lower storey. Other police officers were there, all rightly taking cover. My father thought he must get into the house at once, and found the front door open. He accordingly made his way stealthily through it, but a sub-inspector foolishly followed him with an electric torch which flashed behind my father's head. This, of course, only served to show him up and make him a perfect target. The gunman proceeded to take full advantage of this and fired four shots at his head, silhouetted, as it was, against the wall of the house. By incredible luck all four shots just missed their mark. A drawing taken next day of the holes in the wall made by the bullets showed that they had missed my father's head by less than an inch on either side. Had any one of these landed, he must have been killed. As it was he was unhurt and was able to get across the courtyard to the foot of the gunman's stairway. That fellow then came down the stairs, holding out his hands with a revolver in each, and said, "Sir, I surrender". Soon afterwards the under-ground movement collapsed for the time being.